7/21

Voice

IN THE AMERICAN WEST

Andy Wilkinson
Series Editor

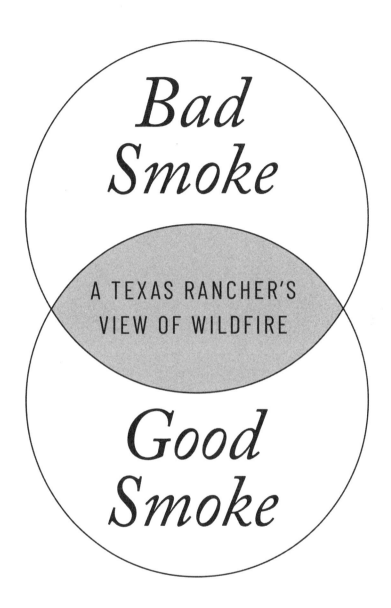

Bad Smoke

A TEXAS RANCHER'S VIEW OF WILDFIRE

Good Smoke

JOHN R. ERICKSON

TEXAS TECH UNIVERSITY PRESS

This book is typeset in Adobe Caslon Pro. The paper used in this book meets the
minimum requirements of ANSI/NISO Z39.48-1992 (R1997). ∞
Designed by Hannah Gaskamp
Cover photograph by Laurie Ezzell Brown, *The Canadian Record*

Library of Congress Cataloging-in-Publication Data

Names: Erickson, John R., 1943– author.
Title: Bad Smoke, Good Smoke: A Texas Rancher's View of Wildfire / John R.
Erickson.
Other titles: Voice in the American West.
Description: Lubbock, Texas: Texas Tech University Press, [2021] | Series: Voice
in the American West | Includes bibliographical references and index. | Summary:
"A description of two 'megafires' (in 2006 and 2017) in the Texas Panhandle, along
with accounts from researchers who study range management, climate, and fire; an
exploration of the symbiotic relationship ranchers have with controlled burning"—
Provided by publisher.
Identifiers: LCCN 2020051141 | ISBN 978-1-68283-087-1 (cloth)
ISBN 978-1-68283-088-8 (ebook)
Subjects: LCSH: Wildfires—Texas—Texas Panhandle—History—21st century.
| Ranchers—Texas—Texas Panhandle. | Range management—Texas—Texas
Panhandle. | Wildfires—Prevention and control.
Classification: LCC SD421.32.T4 E75 2021 | DDC 363.37/9097648—dc23
LC record available at https://lccn.loc.gov/2020051141

Printed in the United States of America
20 21 22 23 24 25 26 27 28 / 9 8 7 6 5 4 3 2 1
Texas Tech University Press
Box 41037
Lubbock, Texas 79409-1037 USA
800.832.4042
ttup@ttu.edu
www.ttupress.org

I would like to dedicate this book to the hundreds of angels who helped Kris and me endure the losses we suffered in 2017, with special thanks to Scot, Tina, and Mark Erickson and George and Karen Chapman. Bless you all!

Contents

PART 2

Introduction

RANCHING IS SOMETHING MY MOTHER'S family was doing in Texas as far back as 1858. It was something I wanted to do as a boy and something I came back to after six years of attending universities and seeing the bright lights of New York City and Boston. It has been one of the passions of my life and the only thing I seem able to write about.

In 1990, I accumulated enough cash to make a down payment on a place of my own and stumbled onto 5,700 acres of rough canyon country in Roberts County, Texas, one of the least populous counties in the state (924 square miles and a population of 929). It had only one incorporated community, the county seat, Miami, with a population of 580, an hour's drive from the ranch.

To my eyes, it was incredibly beautiful, a cowboy's dream, and I did what any cowboy would have done—or wanted to do. I handed over the down payment, signed a big note at the bank, and spent a dozen years sweating over paying off the land.

I gave it the name of my great-grandfather's M-Cross brand, registered in Crosby County in 1887, and for the next twenty-seven years the ranch and I suffered together through every dry spell and shared the joy of every drop of rain.

That's where I was on October 22, 2017, a quiet Sunday afternoon. My wife Kris was at one end of our modular home, working on a quilt, and I was in the bedroom, reading. The chirp of my cell phone interrupted the silence. It was Jim Nicholson, our neighbor on the Parsell ranch.

He said that someone had called him and reported smoke west of us. He wondered if I knew anything about it. I didn't but told him I would check it out. Jim and I had gone through a big wildfire in March and were very sensitive to reports of smoke.

When I stepped out the door, Rosie, our red heeler, raced to the Polaris Ranger and dived into her usual spot on the front seat. We drove up the caprock to a high point where we had a good view of the flat prairie country north of the Canadian River.

I saw the column of gray-white smoke off to the northwest, which stirred jagged memories of the March fires that swept across the northeastern Panhandle. But this one appeared to be an intentional burn of CRP (Conservation Reserve Program) grass or corn stalks. With the calm wind, it posed no threat to our pastures, fences, livestock, or home, and in fact it was making our property safer from fire by reducing the supply of dry fuel. On a bad fire day, with screaming winds, the burned ground would stop a fire before it got to us.

As Rosie and I drove back down into the valley, I remembered something a range management specialist had said, that property owners in the windswept, fire-prone Southern Plains must adapt to fire and learn to use it as a management tool. Part of that process involves changing the way we respond to smoke. There's bad smoke and there's good smoke.

It struck me that *Bad Smoke, Good Smoke* would be an appropriate title for this book, because my story begins with the bad smoke of two very destructive wildfires and evolves into a discussion of prescribed burning, a range-management technique that might allow citizens of the plains to coexist with a highly flammable prairie.

Until recent times, it had never occurred to me that smoke on the horizon could be anything but *bad*.

The wildfires of 2006 and 2017 introduced citizens of the high plains to "megafires," the National Weather Service's term for fires that burn more than 100,000 acres. This was a new and scary dimension of reality: fires that were huge and driven by powerful winds; fires that burned hundreds of thousands of acres, destroyed homes, threatened entire towns, killed people and livestock, and continued burning for days.

The fires of 2006 burned over a million acres in the Texas Panhandle. The rate of spread was an unprecedented 72 km in nine hours, resulting in losses unsurpassed in Texas recorded history: twelve people dead, 4,000 cattle lost, eighty-nine structures and 2,000 miles of fencing destroyed (Lindley 2017, 2).

The Perryton fire of 2017 burned 318,000 acres and was only one of many wildfires on March 6 that covered 1.2 million acres of land in Texas, Oklahoma, and Kansas.

These were landmark events that are etched onto the memory of an entire generation and will be passed down to the next. They made the old-time methods of fighting fire with shovels, wet gunnysacks, and ranch spray rigs a pathetic joke.

I had a ringside seat to both fires, and in part 1 of this book I attempt to express what I saw and how I felt about them. I wasn't riding a fire truck in the middle of the night. I wasn't injured and did nothing heroic. I was merely close enough to smell the smoke and to be in some danger and happened to be a professional wordsmith with the skills and discipline to record the events.

Chapter 1 is a daily log of what I was doing and seeing during the five days we were stalked by the 2006 fire. I didn't think of it as an essay or a piece of "writing," only a report for friends who were concerned about our safety. I sent out daily reports via email. We had no landline phone, so we connected to the internet through a satellite service.

At some point, after the fires had died out, it occurred to me that John Graves, the beloved Texas author and a friend of mine, would enjoy reading my notes. He was a careful observer of land and livestock, and we had corresponded on a fairly regular basis since I visited his ranch, Hard Scrabble, in 1973.

He didn't use email and was still banging out his letters on a manual typewriter, so I printed out my fire notes and sent them by regular mail. (Toward the end of his life, John did start using a computer.) His reply came a week later, and I was surprised by his enthusiastic response. He said I should send the piece to *Texas Monthly*. I didn't know anyone at *TM* or supposed they had much interest in the Panhandle, so I sent it to *American Cowboy*, for whom I had done some writing.

The editor, Jesse Mullins, liked it. When I told him I would be participating in a big wildfire benefit concert organized by singer-songwriter Michael Martin Murphey, he asked me to do an article on that, too. He ran both pieces in 2006 and entered them as one submission in the National Cowboy Museum's Wrangler Awards contest. To my surprise, it won Best Magazine Article of 2006. I have used those articles, with changes and additions, in chapter 1.

Chapter 2 serves as a bridge between the fires of 2006 and 2017, and chapter 3 is the daily log I kept during and after the 2017 fire, when Kris and I lost our home and 90 percent of the pastureland on the ranch. It is the longest section of the book, and I divided it up by days and sometimes by topics. It is a record of what I was doing, seeing, and thinking after the March 6 fire.

My experience in keeping notes during the 2006 fire taught me that the accumulation of small details in recording such an event brings it to life. At the time, those details seemed insignificant, but taken together they tell a story behind the story we see on the evening news. Those details must be captured fresh or they will evaporate from memory.

I have included an account of the tragic death of our granddaughter in May of that year. I debated about whether or not to add this material because, strictly speaking, it wasn't part of our experience with the fire. And yet it *was* because it added a deep, personal layer of grief on top of the loss we had already suffered.

In chapter 4, I move to November and evaluate the ranch's recovery from the fire and Kris's and my efforts to restore some order into our lives. By that time we were back on the ranch, living in a modular home, and thought we were done with fires for a while. I had written the first draft of this book and believed it was finished.

Unfortunately, the story didn't come to a tidy end, and chapters 5 and 6 record our anxiety on the first and second anniversaries of the 2017 fire. The winter/spring of 2018 and 2019 brought more fire outbreaks and warnings and an increased awareness that fire might have become a normal part of life on the Southern Plains.

In part 2, I take a more analytical approach and try to place fire into a broader perspective, combining my own observations with the research of Stephen J. Pyne, Michael Kodas, Katharine Hayhoe, J. Evetts Haley, Julie Courtwright, Henry Wright, and others. I was surprised that there was a fairly large body of literature about fires, and those books and articles helped me understand a rancher's relationship with this ancient force.

Chapters 7 and 8 address the questions that came out of our experience with the fires of 2006 and 2017. Why, in the space of eleven years, did we see two of the biggest prairie fires in modern times? Had West Texas ever seen such extraordinary fires? What caused them, and was it part of a new pattern?

Chapter 9 takes up a question that has been on the minds of landowners in Texas, Oklahoma, New Mexico, and Kansas since the 2017 fires: Where do we go from here? It seems clear that we must find ways of adapting our lives and grazing practices to the natural patterns of fire, which will have to include prescribed burning of pastureland—good smoke.

I have used chapter 10 as a kind of epilogue, an occasion to reassess the decision I made around three o'clock on March 6, 2017, to drop everything and run from the fire. My conclusion: If we were faced with the same circumstances today, I would make the same decision.

I am grateful to Dr. Alex Hunt and B. A. Stewart of West Texas A&M University for helping in my research; also Todd Lindley, Dr. Ron Sosebee, Keith Blair, and Skip Hollandsworth.

I would also like to thank the following people who read early versions of the book and offered comments: Kris Erickson, Scot Dykema, Mike Harter, Martha Marmaduke, Owen Marmaduke, George Clay, Doug Wilkens, Marvin Olasky, Dr. Michael Klein, Nathan Dahlstrom, Del Lemon, and Nikki Georgacakis. I am especially grateful to Joanna Conrad, my editor at TTU Press, who gave me excellent advice on how to sharpen the story, and I appreciate the hard work and patience of editors Travis Snyder and Christie Perlmutter.

Finally, I would like to express my thanks to the hundreds of friends and family members who helped Kris and me through a difficult time, blessing us with meals, clothes, furniture, hay, labor, cards, letters, donations, and hugs at the grocery store.

August 2020
M-Cross Ranch
Roberts County, Texas

Bad Smoke

Good Smoke

PART I

THE
WILDFIRES
OF 2006
AND 2017

CHAPTER 1

The Fires of March 2006

MY FIRST EXPOSURE TO PRAIRIE FIRES came in 1978, when I was working on one of the Barby family ranches in the Oklahoma Panhandle. One night, I was called out of bed to fight a fire on Leland Barby's ranch, north of the Beaver River. It had been started by lightning, and I joined ten other cowboys to battle it. We shoveled dirt on smoldering cow chips and used wet gunnysacks to beat out the flames in the burning grass.

As prairie fires go, it was pretty tame and even had the feel of a social occasion. All the cowboys from six Barby ranches got together in the middle of the night, did brave things, and swapped stories around the water can, then returned to our wives, reeking of smoke and feeling heroic. Our efforts might have helped control the spread of the fire, but the fact is, rain put it out.

One afternoon in the summer of 1979, while I was working on the LZ ranch south of Perryton, Texas, lightning started a fire on the Parnell brothers' ranch, which joined us on the south. Tom Ellzey and I saw white smoke, grabbed shovels and gunnysacks, and went to help. Again, it wasn't much of a fire and rain shut it down.

In 1990, we bought our M-Cross Ranch in Roberts County, Texas, southeast of Perryton. During the first sixteen years, we had two fires on our place. The first came during a rainstorm, when lightning struck an oil tank in the east pasture. It blew the tank a hundred yards from its original location and singed some grass, but rain killed the fire.

The second fire occurred at night, and I didn't even know about it until several days later, when I found twenty acres of burned grass. It was another case of lightning starting the fire and rain putting it out.

During that same period, other ranches in our neighborhood (within a thirty-mile radius) had fires. Lightning started a fire in some CRP grass along Highway 281, north of our place. It made a lot of smoke (this was in the summer and the grass was green), but fire units from Perryton and Canadian got it under control.

In 1995, a welder touched off a more serious fire on Boone Pickens's Mesa Vista Ranch, across the Canadian River from us. It moved from southwest to northeast, jumped the river, and burned into the brushy river bottom on two ranches that joined us, the Killebrew and Tandy ranches.

Our place was never in much danger, but Jim and Laura Streeter, who lived in the house on the Tandy ranch, were concerned enough that Laura began loading things into her car. Our daughter Ashley helped her.

That was a scary fire, but motor graders from Roberts and Ochiltree Counties plowed fire guards and got it stopped at North River Road. From start to finish, that fire had a life of about four hours. No houses burned.

Until March 12, 2006, that was the sum total of my experience with prairie fires.

SUNDAY, MARCH 12, 2006

At 10:30 that morning, Kris and I climbed the steps on the south side of the Methodist church in Perryton. I paused and glanced up at the pale sky. The wind was screaming out of the west, a straight, relentless gale in the range of fifty to sixty miles an hour. It was exactly what we didn't need in the Texas Panhandle: another day of hot, dry wind.

I grew up in this country, and windy days in March were no surprise, but there was an ominous quality to this wind. I said to Kris, "No good ever comes from a west wind." I had no idea how prophetic those words would turn out to be.

After church, we ate lunch at a restaurant and headed back to the ranch. Around three o'clock, we came to the caprock, a three-hundred-foot escarpment on the north edge of the wide Canadian River Valley. On a clear day, you could see twenty miles. Today, the air had a dirty-brown color. I assumed it was dust blowing in from New Mexico.

Then we smelled smoke and knew that at least some of that haze was coming from a grass fire, probably far to the west of us. Smoke can travel great distances. In the past, we had gotten smoke from big fires in Mexico and Yellowstone National Park.

We drove on home. Today, it seems incredible that we were so casual at the time.

Around eight that night, our son Scot called from Amarillo. We didn't have television and he knew we hadn't been watching the news. "Dad," he said, "there's a huge fire in Roberts County and you need to find out where it is. If it's close, you'd better get out of that canyon." Our house sat in a deep, tree-lined canyon north of the Canadian River.

We loaded up in our Ford Excursion (Kris, her mother, and I) and drove to a high spot in the east pasture, where we had a good view of the country to the south. There, we saw an astonishing sight, a line of flames that lit up the entire southern horizon and appeared to be fifty miles long. The reports on the radio said that the towns of Miami (our county seat, about twenty-five miles south), Wheeler, Canadian, McLean, and Alanreed were being evacuated.

Since the fire seemed to be south of the river and driven by a west wind, I thought we'd be safe spending the night at the ranch. In the months and years that followed, I began to realize that in such dry conditions, our canyon could be a death trap if the wind shifted, as it often does in March, and as it did in days to come.

We had an abundance of big cedar trees in our canyon, many of them thirty feet tall, and some stood dangerously close to the house. In normal times, we saw them as objects of beauty, but they were also *fuel*. We should have left the ranch.

I woke up many times in the night, went out on the porch, and checked for smoke. If I had smelled smoke, we would have evacuated, but there was no strong smell and the wind subsided in the night.

MONDAY, MARCH 13

Monday morning, I drove up to a lookout point in the east pasture and listened to the news on the radio. It was grim. The fire had started with a downed power line on the 6666 ranch south of Borger and swept across the northern Panhandle.

Another fire began on I-40, near McLean, and burned tens of thousands of acres in the Red River drainage. The two fires together burned over a million acres of rangeland. News reports said that seven people had died (the final count climbed to twelve), homes and thousands of miles of fence had been destroyed, and nobody could guess the loss of livestock.

I could see that big fires were still burning on the south side of the river. Although I couldn't judge their exact location, they appeared to be south of the Payne and McMordie ranches along the river. I tried to call some of the neighbors on my cell phone, but the service was out. Later, I learned that the fire had burned the power lines to the tower.

Around four o'clock, several Forest Service tanker planes began dropping red fire retardant around a house on the Payne ranch. It was partially shrouded in smoke, but it appeared that the fire had been contained and that it wouldn't make it into the heavy vegetation in the riverbed.

I felt that the worst had passed for us, if not for those ranchers further south. The weather forecast was calling for a day of fairly calm winds on Tuesday.

TUESDAY, MARCH 14

In the morning, I drove out of the canyon and scanned the country south of us. I saw small plumes of smoke, but it appeared that we might be all right, except that the weather forecast called for strong winds out of the southwest on Wednesday. That was a bad direction for us.

In the afternoon, I drove up the river and talked to Starla Nicholson on the C Bar C ranch. She caught me up on all the news, including the report that three burned bodies had been found north of Miami, oil field workers who had gotten trapped in their car.

WEDNESDAY, MARCH 15

I got up at 4:30 and drove out of the valley to a high spot. I saw only one glow of fire on the Payne ranch. By ten o'clock, the winds had picked up again and created an eerie scene. The air was filled with haze, so that it was hard to determine whether fresh smoke or a mix of ash and dust were blowing off the burned country to the south.

I didn't want to take any chances. Randy Wilson, my son-in-law, took the day off and came out to help me. We spent all day cutting down big cedar trees near the house and using a skid-steer tractor to drag them into the bed of a dry pond. Some of those trees had stood for fifty years or more and I hated to cut them down.

Around four o'clock, Jason Pelham, a cowboy on the McMordie ranch, called to say that the fire had roared back to life and had jumped the river. Moments later, a sheriff's car came up our road, its lights flashing. The deputy recommended that we evacuate.

By this time, we could see billows of smoke to the east, above the canyon rim. The fire appeared to be on the Adams ranch that joined us on the east, way too close for comfort.

Kris had about fifteen minutes to decide what she wanted to save from the house we had occupied for fifteen years, then Randy and I led her and her mother through thirteen miles of pasture roads to Highway 70.

At that point, I didn't know the extent of the fire or whether we might find more fires between our ranch and the highway. If we encountered fire, we might be trapped in the valley. But we were lucky; all the fires were east of us.

The radio news said that fire crews were massing in southeast Ochiltree County, where they hoped to stop the fire when it came out of the canyons north of the river. Randy and I drove to a high spot in the east pasture and watched as the fire raged across the Adams ranch. From the high ground, we could see that it had come within 300 yards of our east fence and was on a path to the northeast, away from our place.

After dark, we could see the flashing lights of emergency vehicles all across the wide Canadian River Valley and up on the flats to the north. I didn't count them, but there must have been at least seventy-five trucks. I didn't know it at the time, but we were watching the largest single mobilization of firefighters in Texas history, with more than 700 professional and volunteer firemen involved.

Clearly, the people who knew about fires were taking this one very seriously, but there wasn't much a fire truck could do to stop a fast-moving wildfire. The forward surge had to be stopped by fireguards and backfires. Experienced crews stayed out of its path, waited for the initial charge of the fire to pass, then went in and put out the lingering flames, smoldering cow chips, yucca, and mesquite trees.

While we watched, the fire raced northward and entered Bourbonese Canyon on the Adams ranch. This was the biggest canyon in the area, very similar to the canyons on our ranch, only longer and wider. It contained an abundance of big cedar trees as well as cottonwood, elm, hackberry, and soapberry. It was loaded with dry fuel.

We couldn't see the fire directly when it got into the canyon, but the red-orange glow that showed above the canyon rims was spectacular and frightening. A massive column of billowing gray smoke rose above the fire and disappeared into the night sky.

Randy and I had loaded the pickup with sleeping bags, food, and water. We didn't know where we would be sleeping, if we would make it back to the house, or if there would be any house left. We made our way down a dark, twisting road from the high country, drove to the barn, and loaded my tractor onto a flatbed trailer. It ran on rubber tracks, like a bulldozer, and worked well in rough and sandy country.

We hauled it over to a pasture on the Adams ranch that joined us. There, we saw fire burning through catclaw and cedar brush on the sides of several big mesas, sending up clouds of black and gray smoke. It was moving against the wind in a long line toward our mesa pasture.

At some point (events and time had begun to blur), we encountered a volunteer fire crew of cowboys from the C Bar C ranch, parked in the darkness on Hank's Road. Inside the pickup were Billy DeArmond, Dave Nicholson, Clint DeArmond, and Jody Chisum. For three days they had been fighting fire on the south side of the river and now they had brought their ranch's fire truck over to the north side.

They were in good spirits, but their eyes showed fatigue. We talked for a while, then they were called down to North River Road.

Randy and I stayed to monitor the fire on the western front, and we were the only ones there. Most of the crews and equipment were working the biggest fires to the east of us on the Adams ranch. Then two fire rigs from the Gruver Volunteer Fire Department arrived, including two men I knew: Jake and Benny McCullough, owners of Diamond M Water Well Service. They had worked all day on windmills. Now they would be fighting fire all night.

They drove out into the pasture toward the line of fire, quite an act of courage. It was dark, those men didn't know this pasture, and the terrain was rough, even for a four-wheel drive vehicle. They drove along the line of fire and sprayed it with water. That killed the flames so that I could go behind them in the track loader, knocking down smoldering mesquite trees and covering them with dirt.

They made their way along the base of the mesa and somehow managed to keep from getting stuck or ruining a tire. Randy and I kept a close eye on them, in case we had to pull them out with the tractor.

Fire crews on the flats north of the valley had thrown up fireguards and backfires to stop the blaze when it came out of the canyons and to prevent it from spreading into an ocean of tall grass in Lipscomb County to the northeast. That would have put five small towns in jeopardy. In days to come, I saw that they had graded wide fireguards three miles ahead of the blaze, an indication of just how worried they were.

About eleven o'clock, the wind shifted around to the northwest. If the wind hadn't changed, I'm not sure the fire could have been stopped. Once the wind changed, the fire turned and started burning back through the Adams and Parsell ranches, this time moving southeast, through rough canyons and mesas. Randy and I kept watch until 2 and went to bed. It had been a long day and I was shot.

THURSDAY, MARCH 16

We got up around seven and drove up to a high spot to check the situation. The winds had died down in the night but were fairly strong out of the northeast. Several big fires still burned around Tandy Mesa, about two miles east of my place, as well as dozens of smaller fires across the valley.

During the morning, big four-engine airplanes from the Forest Service swooped down and dropped loads of chemical retardant on these fires, putting out the worst of them. A big Chinook helicopter was also working the fire. It would hover over a pond or stock tank, lower a snorkel, and suck up water, then discharge it over a hot spot.

Our sons, Mark and Scot, came from Amarillo to see how we were doing and to survey the damage. Around noon, Mark and I spotted a cedar tree burning in one of the Adams pastures. It had smoldered for at least a day and the wind had brought it back to life. We were carrying shovels and a chainsaw in the pickup, so we cut it down and spent an hour covering it with sand. Later, it occurred to me how silly that might have appeared to an observer: two men huffing and puffing to put out a little blaze in the midst of 900,000 blackened acres.

The fires in the roughest parts of the valley burned all day, until they ran out of fuel. During the day we saw crews and equipment from Perryton, Canadian, Higgins, Hoover, Gruver, Tarrant County (300 miles to the south), and even some Forest Service crews from Oregon. Other firefighters had come from South Dakota, towns in Oklahoma, the Dallas area, and Midland.

FRIDAY, MARCH 17

A slow sizzle of rain began to fall in the morning, and for the first time in five days we felt that the monster had finally been killed. Kris and her mother returned home in the evening. The damp weather continued on into Saturday and Sunday. On Monday, we received a light snow.

To the south of us lay the death and destruction of the worst wildfire in Texas history. We had survived, but the memory was not likely to fade.

THE WILDFIRE BENEFIT CONCERT

The first week in April, I received an email from Michael Martin Murphey. He was trying to put together two benefit concerts in Amarillo to raise money for victims of the

Panhandle wildfires. He had organized a private benefit on Good Friday and a big public concert the following day.

He had gotten commitments from a number of performers, including Don Edwards, Red Steagall, and Baxter Black. Would I be willing to help? I said I would be honored to participate—unless the Canadian River Valley was on fire again. If that happened, I would be trying to protect my home and ranch.

This was not idle speculation. The one inch of moisture that had finally killed the big fires in March had been sucked away by relentless southwest winds, and suddenly the Panhandle found itself in danger again. In early April, a fire broke out in the northeast part of Amarillo and destroyed fourteen homes. Another fire swept through ranch country north of Amarillo and burned 50,000 acres. Still another burned 22,000 acres in Lipscomb County, just thirty miles northeast of our ranch. The nightmare continued.

On Good Friday, April 14, I made the hundred-mile drive to Amarillo. Between the Canadian River and Pampa, I drove through a twenty-mile stretch of burned ranch land on Highway 70. That poor barren country was now being flogged by the same kind of wind that had driven the original fires on March 13. An ugly haze of dust and ash filled the air.

I drove past two men who were working near the highway, repairing a stretch of burned fence on Joe Hutchison's Bridle Bit Ranch. I knew Joe and had worked a few brandings with him. He was skilled with a horse and a rope, a hard-working man who had built up a cattle operation in Roberts and Gray Counties.

I heard that he had lost twenty sections of grass to the fires—12,800 acres—and now he was working daylight to dark to keep his cattle fed with round bales and trying to rebuild his fences.

MMM, RED STEAGALL, AND DON EDWARDS

The Friday night benefit program was held at the home of Dr. Keith Bjork in the north part of Amarillo. I was one of the first performers to arrive and made my way to the spacious backyard, where several men were setting up microphones and speakers.

Michael Martin Murphey was standing near the swimming pool, where we exchanged greetings. "Murph," as his friends called him, had organized the Friday night benefit to raise money for volunteer fire departments in little towns across the Panhandle. They had been fighting fires for a month. They were exhausted and their budgets depleted. It was a worthy cause—as I knew very well.

Red Steagall arrived around 5:30. I hadn't seen him in years; he appeared not to have aged, except that his once-red beard had turned snow-white. He had the same proud stature and piercing gaze, with smoky blue eyes that cut through the surface and went to things deeper.

Later, when he sang about ranch people in the West, his voice had the crack of conviction. His years of performing had not diminished his affection for the land and the people who worked it, sentiments he expressed so well in his songs, poems, books, and radio programs.

While Red and I were talking, I glanced toward the western horizon (a habit that had become ingrained in recent weeks) and saw a white ghost of smoke rising in the sky, a grassfire west of the city. I nudged Red and said, "Look at that." He squinted toward the smoke and for a few moments we both pondered this nasty little irony, watching a grassfire at a grassfire benefit concert.

After a period of silence, he said, "We've interfered with nature's plan, haven't we? Fire is nature's way of cleansing herself, but we get in the way."

That fire served as a reminder that until we received some rain, there was no safe haven in the Texas Panhandle. City people probably didn't feel the threat, but anyone who had seen the March fires up close could imagine what fire might do if it ever got into those tightly packed suburban neighborhoods on the west side of Amarillo.

The thought of whole towns burning had never entered my mind before the spring of 2006, but now it had become a frightening possibility. Downstate, fires had wiped out the little towns of Ringgold and Cross Plains, and our fires in March had come very close to several small towns in the eastern Panhandle.

The Amarillo Fire Department must have responded quickly to the blaze we were observing; in thirty minutes most of the smoke had dissipated, much to the relief of those of us who were watching. It wouldn't have been funny, abandoning our fire benefit because of a fire.

Don Edward and his wife arrived around six o'clock. I had met Don years before at the National Cowboy Symposium in Lubbock and had seen him a few years later at the cowboy poetry gathering at Elko, Nevada. He was the same man onstage and off: quiet, gentle, modest, witty, and as honest as an old pair of boots.

He had gone his own way in the music business, singing old-time cowboy songs, and had found an audience in busy, noisy modern America. He wasn't a "star" in the usual sense of the word, and neither were the rest of us. Murph and Red had gotten close enough to the big lights to feel their heat but gave them up and went back to quieter places. Like Don, they steered their own course, taking the music they loved to the people they cared about.

That's why they were there in Amarillo, raising money for firefighters and burned-out ranchers, instead of attending a cocktail party in Nashville or Los Angeles. I was proud to be with them.

THE SATURDAY CONCERT

I spent the night at the Ambassador Hotel, at ten stories one of the tallest buildings in Amarillo. When I awoke Saturday morning, I heard an odd sound outside the sealed windows. The wind was blowing again, hard.

I leaped out of bed, went to the window, and scanned the sleeping city, looking for smoke. I saw none and felt relieved, but the presence of that strong southwest wind ensured that I would be thinking of little else during the day. I had left my wife, mother-in-law, and two grandchildren at the ranch, on a day when the wolf was howling for fresh meat.

The Saturday concert was to be held at Amarillo's Globe News Center for the Performing Arts, home of the Amarillo Symphony, and it had been sold out for days. I arrived around 10 a.m. and talked to a couple of friends from Lipscomb County, J. W. Beeson and R. J. Vandygriff, who were also on the program. Beeson was a saddle maker and cowboy poet, R. J. a professional musician.

It didn't take long for our conversation to turn to the fires. I learned that both men had been involved in fighting the big fires in March, across the river from my place. They told some harrowing tales about racing their fire truck through the flames; both still had burns to show for it.

Beeson had driven over to Amarillo that morning. I asked if he'd seen any smoke on the way. He nodded. "Looked like there was a big one down around Wheeler. Some of the boys on our fire department had tickets to the concert but they decided they'd better stay home, with this wind."

The concert got started at 1:45, with the introduction of dignitaries and honored guests, including representatives from Farm Bureau who had helped coordinate the fundraising efforts. MMM opened the show, performing with the Amarillo Symphony. They did several songs, then "Wildfire," the song for which he is best known.

The song's title had an eerie resonance for an audience of Panhandle folks who had learned a lot more about wildfires than they ever wanted to know. Another macabre twist occurred backstage when a tight-lipped man hung up his cell phone and muttered, "Good grief, they're evacuating neighborhoods in southwest Amarillo because of fires!" He wasn't joking.

"Wildfire" was a great song when MMM first recorded it, and it was just as fine when he performed it with the Amarillo Symphony. It began with an unusual riff on the piano—very nice, but not exactly western or "cowboy." Murphey told me that he borrowed it from the Russian composer, Aleksandr Scriabin; that Saturday it was being played by an accomplished concert pianist named John Bayless, who grew up in the Panhandle town of Borger. The fire that came close to burning my ranch in March had started on a ranch near Borger.

Murphey, Bayless, and the Amarillo Symphony made beautiful music and the crowd loved them. Backstage, however, the people who were managing the concert began to fret that the show was already running long and might go on for five or six hours. Still to go: Don Edwards, a group called Palo Duro, R. J. Vandygriff, Mike Siler, J. W. Beeson, Richard Bowden and Lucky Boyd, me, Baxter Black, Red Steagall, then the finale number with everyone on stage singing "Home On The Range."

I saw Paul Sadler, Murphey's road manager, and told him that he could take me off the program, if my fifteen minutes would help him keep to the schedule. He said no, but if I could cut my time down to ten minutes, that would help.

I didn't tell Paul, but I would have been glad to give up my spot. I found it hard to think about anything but the fire danger at my ranch. I paced and prowled until, around four o'clock, I went out and did a ten-minute reading from one of the Hank the Cowdog books. I took a bow and hurried offstage.

There, in the half-darkness, I saw Baxter Black, as trim as an eel, wearing a smile beneath his splendid mustache and waiting his turn to perform.

Baxter and I had been friends since the early eighties. In those days, cowboy poetry was still in its infancy, and most Americans, including me, had adjusted to the notion that poetry was a dead literary form, exterminated by unhappy scribes who had stripped it of meter, rhyme, humor, joy, and anything else you might want in a poem.

But along came Baxter, who had spent his college days studying bovine anatomy instead of the howls of postmodern literature. He started writing poetry that came from the heart. He made people *laugh* and sold his books to an audience that was beginning to suspect that poetry wasn't as dead as we had thought.

And here he was in Amarillo, helping raise money for folks who had taken a beating from the fires. He had come all the way from Arizona to help. Red had come from Ft. Worth, Boyd and Bowden from East Texas, Don Edwards from Hico, MMM from New Mexico. It was a noble thing for them to do, exactly the sort of thing citizens of the West have always done.

I didn't stay for Baxter's performance or the rest of the concert but jumped into my pickup and headed back to Roberts County. All the way there, I scanned the horizon for smoke and didn't relax until I drove into Pickett Canyon and found that my house was still standing. We had made it through another day.

On Sunday morning, Kris and I attended the Easter service at our church in Perryton, which included a ritual called the Flowering of the Cross. Every member of the congregation walked to the front and placed a fresh flower on a bare cross, transforming it into an object of breathtaking beauty, a symbol of hope and rebirth.

Our ravaged country would have to wait for rebirth, but we still had hope that one of these days the rain would fall and the grass would come.

CHAPTER 2

Between the Fires

SEVERAL MONTHS AFTER THE WILDFIRES of 2006, I was driving through the Killebrew ranch, which joined our M-Cross ranch on the south. I saw a pickup trailer rig parked on the side of the road. A saddled horse stood in the trailer.

Burk Adcock, my neighbor who leased the Killebrew place, got out of the pickup. He wore faded jeans and a well-traveled felt hat pulled down to the tops of his ears. It was the hat of a man accustomed to working in the wind.

We met in the road. He gave me an easy smile and we shook hands. His fingers were thick and rough, the texture of the road at our feet.

Burk and I shared two miles of common fence but seldom ran into each other or talked. Occasionally his cattle or mine walked the cattle guard between us and we had to get things sorted out. Burk was a busy man, with a cattle operation spread out over several Texas counties, but I never doubted that if I ever got into a bind, a call to his cell phone would bring help as fast as he could get there. He knew that I would do the same for him.

We exchanged bits of news (family, grass, cattle), then, inevitably, our conversation turned to the Big Fire. That

Sunday afternoon, March 12, Burk and his wife Kim were horseback on the Killebrew place, riding pastures and checking cattle. Burk noticed a dark smudge in the sky, south of the river. He kept his eye on it. It grew larger and darker, and he said, "You know, I think that's a fire."

Both he and his father ran cattle on pastures across the river, and it appeared that the fire, if that's what it was, might be heading their way. Burk told Kim they'd better load the horses and go check.

By the time they crossed the Canadian River Bridge on Highway 70, they knew it was a fire, a bad one, and Burk's dad's cattle appeared to be right in its path. When they reached one of the pastures, west of Miami, Burk stopped the pickup and unloaded his horse. He told Kim to drive home and prepare for a fire. He would open gates and try to push the cattle to safe ground and get home as soon as he could.

Kim drove away (with a heavy heart, I'm sure) while Burk set out horseback. Smoke filled the air and he knew the fire was getting close, but he thought he would have enough time to get the cattle moved.

What he didn't know, couldn't have known, was that this was a kind of fire he'd never seen. By the time he realized it, his biggest problem wasn't saving cattle but saving himself. When he caught his first glimpse of yellow flames leaping through billows of smoke, it dawned on him that he couldn't outrun it. The flames would be on him in a matter of minutes.

He turned his horse and galloped to a ravine that was ten feet deep. In the bottom of the ravine, he dived out of the saddle, took down his rope, and snugged the loop around the horse's left front hock. He tied up the leg with a half-hitch over the saddle horn and pulled the horse's head around to the right, bedding him down on his side.

By this time, the sun had been swallowed by a pall of dark smoke and he could hear the roar of the fire. He hunkered down and held the horse's head in the pulled-back position, to keep him from thrashing and injuring himself. The roar of the fire filled his ears and the air above his head grew as hot as an oven . . . then it was gone. He had missed death by ten feet.

Burk told me that story in the middle of a dirt road, delivering it in the same calm, understated manner he might have used to describe changing a flat tire. It was the voice of a man who didn't want to call attention to himself, who didn't need to convince anyone he had done something special. But I recognized it for what it was: a tale of extraordinary courage and resilience.

I never forgot it and wondered how many people were lucky enough to hear Burk tell it—probably not many. Eleven years later, I incorporated the story into a Hank book, *The Case of the Monster Fire*. Most of the incidents in the Hank stories come from my own experience, but this one belonged to Burk Adcock.

Twelve people didn't have Burk's presence of mind, or weren't as lucky, and they perished in the fire. Three oil field workers tried to outrun the blaze in a pickup and got trapped. A volunteer firefighter was crushed when his fire truck overturned in a pasture. Ranch people died trying to defend their homes and livestock with garden hoses and gunnysacks, the pitiful weapons they had used in the past to extinguish trash-barrel fires and lazy blazes caused by lightning.

The thing they all had in common was that nothing in their experience had prepared them for a fire of this magnitude. It was, to borrow a popular cliché, a perfect storm that brought together low humidity (below 15 percent), gale-force wind, a weakness on a utility pole in Hutchinson County, and a sea of tall, brittle grass that, in past years, ranchers had regarded as a blessing.

When the fires were finally extinguished, landowners began dealing with the damage. Ranchers whose pastures had been burned had to buy feed and hay for their stock, then move their cattle to other pastures, giving the burned pastures a season to recover. Charred fences had to be rebuilt at a cost of $10,000 to $15,000 per mile. For some ranchers, these added expenses were catastrophic. They either took on more debt or went out of business.

George Chapman, a friend who ranched near McLean, lost a ranch house and everything it contained. Nothing survived. He had to rebuild 180 miles of fence, suffered substantial damage and death loss to his registered Bonsmara cattle, and had to remove hundreds more from scorched pastures and relocate them on leased ranches far away.

His greatest regret, after the loss of the house and cattle, was the destruction of the big, graceful cottonwood trees on his property. Today, young cottonwoods are coming back along the creeks, but it will take decades for them to replace the ones that were killed by the intense heat of the fires. Those beautiful trees died but didn't burn, and their bleached skeletons remain to this day, a stark reminder of a week that George and his neighbors will never forget.

But the resilience of this prairie country is extraordinary. Out of devastation came fresh growth. Out of death came new life. Fire is just as much a part of God's design as the rainfall that washes away the cinders. Life moves on.

Five years later, the land that burned was in better condition than before the fires. Before the appearance of modern ranching operations, prairie fires provided a natural method of improving grassland, disposing of old growth and dead wood, and controlling the spread of invader plants such as mesquite, cedar, cactus, and yucca.

The fires of 2006 got a good kill on the cedar and yucca but only top-killed the rugged mesquite. Much of it sprouted back from roots that were undamaged by the fast-moving flames.

The land recovered, but those of us who lived through wildfires of 2006 were changed. We had acquired a deep animal fear of what fire can do to the fragile artifacts of our civilization. I noticed it in myself and saw it in my neighbors. In dry times, when the wind cranked up, our eyes scanned the horizon. The faintest smell of grass smoke sent us to high ground, calling neighbors on cell phones. "Where's that smoke coming from?"

Before the fires, we were proud to show off acres of waving sideoats grama and little bluestem grass and to credit ourselves with good stewardship of the land. Now, it was hard to forget that every stem and blade of grass can become *fuel*—meat and potatoes for the kind of monster we saw in 2006.

Before the fire, I was giving serious consideration to doing some controlled burns on my ranch. My country needed a good cleansing that only a fire can provide, but I couldn't bring myself to drop a match into a clump of grass. I just couldn't do it.

THE DROUGHT

In the years 2011–2014, we weren't thinking much about wildfires. Our country, and most of the central United States, had fallen into the grip of a vicious drought, one of the worst on record. We received no spring rains in 2011 and our pastures were bare. My cattle were eating weeds, tree branches, and yucca leaves—anything that showed a trace of green.

You couldn't have started a prairie fire with gasoline. There was nothing to burn.

We moved fifty cows to a place near Shawnee, Oklahoma, but the drought followed and we ended up selling thin cows on a drought market. Everybody from Montana to Mexico was selling cows and buying hay to feed the ones that remained.

We sold another bunch that had been running on leased pasture, and we went through the winter of 2013–2014 with forty cows on 5,700 acres. Even that small number was too many.

In May 2014, we hadn't gotten our spring rains and I was about ready to sell the last of our cows when the rain started. We received 1.85" near the end of May, 6.50" in June, 8.75" in July, and ended the year with 27", six inches above our average of 21 per year. The year 2015 brought 32", and 2016 was a real boomer with 34 inches.

Most of the 2016 moisture came in gentle rains, soaking into the ground rather than washing it away, and it replenished the subsoil moisture we had lost in the drought. Even so, we had spots of 20–30 acres where the good buffalo-grass turf had been killed, and it came back in weeds. I had always heard that you couldn't kill buffalo grass, but that was incorrect. A combination of drought and extreme cold will kill it at the roots, and it is very slow to come back.

August 2016 was the wettest month I had ever recorded on our ranch. We had water in the ponds and water standing in the ditches, and most of the pastures had grass that stood knee-high or taller. We had survived the drought, but the memory of the 2006 fires lingered. When I swapped rainfall reports with Burk Adcock, he would arch his brows and say, "We sure have a lot of fuel out there in those pastures."

THE ICE STORM

In September, the rain spigot shut off. We received very little moisture until January, when we got precipitation in a form we didn't want: a two-day assault of freezing rain and ice. A thick layer of ice formed on everything. When I stepped out on the porch, I could hear the crack and pop of cedar limbs breaking in our canyon.

Sunday afternoon at 4:30, our electricity went out. I fitted a pair of ice cleats onto my boots and moved with slow steps to our 45kW diesel generator behind the house. I had been firing it up to keep the battery charged and kept a can of ether close by, in case the diesel engine didn't want to start in the cold. It fired right up, and for the next sixteen days that was our only source of electric power.

The ice storm destroyed hundreds of miles of electric lines, poles, and cross arms in Hansford, Ochiltree, Roberts, and Lipscomb Counties in Texas, and Beaver County in Oklahoma. People who had no backup power supply found themselves living in cold, dark houses. Many of them had to move into motels or temporary housing. You couldn't get a hotel room anywhere in the Texas or Oklahoma Panhandles. It became a regional disaster that very few people outside of our area knew about.

Repair crews, hundreds of workers and hundreds of trucks, came from all over the United States. Nine thousand utility poles had been destroyed. Perryton was without power for several days and cancelled school. The town of Darrouzett was paralyzed for weeks, and the Salvation Army fed people in the school gym. Even the phone service went out when the cellular tower collapsed under the weight of the ice.

The one bright spot in the midst of this destruction was that our area received three inches of slow, soaking rain, and we needed it. As all the survivors of the 2006 fires knew very well, and to quote Burk Adcock, we had a lot of fuel standing out there in the pastures.

I thought the three-inch rain would take us through fire season, until the spring rains started in April and May, but it didn't happen that way. February brought drying wind and no moisture. Then came March.

CHAPTER 3

The Fires of March 2017

MONDAY, MARCH 6, 2017

The weather forecast had warned that high wind was coming, the kind of wind we had learned to fear, 40–50 miles an hour out of the southwest, with gusts to 70. We feared it because the fires of 2006 had taught us what it could do to an ocean of dry prairie grass. Against such a force, we are as helpless as rabbits.

The day began as any other would on our ranch. I got up at 6, drove to my office, and worked on an article. When the sun peeked over the canyon wall, I stepped onto the screened porch and looked out on the beautiful place we had owned for twenty-seven years. The wind was stronger than normal for that time of day, but not terrible. This was March, after all, and in the Texas Panhandle, the wind blows in March.

The National Weather Service, which had developed an uncanny accuracy in predicting bad events, had issued a Red Flag Warning for wind: extreme fire danger.

THE HOUSE

At ten, I left my office and went to the house, a log home with 3,500 square feet of living space. Kris designed it in 1993, working with a log-home company in Montana, and we moved into it in time for Thanksgiving, whenAshley was fifteen and Mark was coming up on eleven. Kris had homeschooled them at the ranch.

Kris had always been a gourmet cook but had spent most of her married life working in small kitchens, so she designed this house around a large kitchen with plenty of work space, a big refrigerator, and a walk-in pantry with three walls of storage. The restaurant-quality Viking stove had four gas burners, two ovens, and a griddle in the center for making pancakes.

There were no inside walls to separate the kitchen from the great room with its big front windows, cathedral ceiling, and fireplace made of native stone. The space flowed together, with the kitchen serving as the focus of the home. That's where people tended to gather, blending two very old and fundamental human endeavors: lively conversation and the preparation of food.

A long dining table occupied the east wall and could seat twelve, or more if we brought in folding chairs, as we often did. It could accommodate a big crowd of family at Thanksgiving, friends from town, or a crew of archeologists who were spending a week with us while they dug sites on the ranch.

Some notable archeologists had sat at that table at one time or another: Doug Boyd, Brett Cruse, Billy Harrison, Rolla Shaller, Charles Frederick, Chris Lintz, Scott Brosowske,

Doug Wilkens, and Richard Drass. Their books and articles on archeology of the Southern Plains would have filled several large library shelves and provided anyone who read them with a fine education on the people who occupied the Canadian River Valley centuries before our ancestors arrived.

We had also fed a lot of first-rate cowboys at that table after a branding or a shipping roundup: Tom Ellzey, Bobby Barnett, Chuck Milner, Dale Githens, Merl Kraft, Hack Coffee, and Nathan Dahlstrom; Lance and Jim Bussard from Lipscomb; Jack and Sam White from the Parsell ranch; Jason Pelham from the Spade ranch and the Abraham brothers from Red Deer Creek; Billy DeArmond, Jody Chissum, and Dave Nicholson from the C Bar C; Burk Adcock from the Killebrew; Brent Clapp from the Adams outfit; and the Erickson boys, Mark and Scot.

And of course the legendary Frankie McWhorter: horse fixer, cowboy, storyteller, and fiddle player. I wrote two books about him and could have written more. Several times we invited friends out for an old-fashioned Saturday night ranch dance. We moved all the furniture against the walls, slid one of Frankie's CDs into the player, and waltzed and two-stepped the night away, remembering our old friend.

It was a very comfortable house, pleasant to the eye and nourishing to the soul. It was filled with Kris's goodness and her love of beautiful things: ten of her handmade quilts, wall hangings, scrapbooks, and photographs of our parents, children, and grandchildren.

SMOKE

I talked to Kris for a while, checked email, and drove to the barn to load sacks of feed. I spent the next two hours pouring out 38-percent protein cubes for cows and yearlings. The cows had started calving; it was always nice to see new life in the ugliest month of the year. The wind was howling now.

I went back to the house, ate a bite of lunch, read for a while, and napped for an hour. I was awakened by the sound of my cell phone ringing. It was our son Mark in Amarillo. He said he was seeing white smoke east of town and wondered if I had noticed anything. Maybe I should check.

I agreed. We didn't have a good view of the horizon in our canyon. In a high wind, a fire could be on us before we knew it. That was a lesson we had learned from the fires of 2006. On days with high fire danger, I made frequent trips to the upper west pasture to check for smoke.

When I started the Ranger, Dixie, our blue heeler, heard the motor and came at a run. She stopped and looked into my eyes. Could she go? "Come on!" She flew into the front seat and licked my face. Riding in the Ranger was always the high point of her day.

When I fed cattle with Dixie, I had to be careful. The dog had been endowed with the powerful instincts of the blue heeler breed: she couldn't resist making a lightning dash at cattle and biting them on the heels, and my shouting had no effect on her.

She was a sweet dog but lacked discipline and self-restraint—my fault. A few weeks before, she had dived out of the Ranger and spooked a cow. The cow ran away from Dixie's slashing attack, bumped into me, and knocked the sack of feed out of my hands. If she had hit me squarely, she could have done some damage. Old guys should try to avoid getting run over by full-grown cows.

We drove a mile south, past the bunkhouse and the barn, turned right, and drove up the long, steep hill that led to the upper west pasture. There, 300 feet above the valley floor, I had an unobstructed view in all directions and could see objects 30–40 miles away.

I saw a thin wisp of white to the southwest, probably from the fire Mark had mentioned, but nothing close to us. The wind was screaming out of the west-southwest, blowing so hard that I could feel it rocking the Ranger.

I drove back down into the valley and parked behind the house, went inside, and told Kris that all was well. My cell phone rang. It was Brian Freelove, who worked for Mewbourne Oil Company and took care of some wells on our place.

"John, a pumper just called and said there's a fire on Ouida Wilson's place."

"That's odd. I was just up on the flats and didn't see any smoke."

"I don't know if it's true, but in this wind, you ought to check." I agreed and thanked him for the call.

Ouida Wilson had died several years before, a charming, beautiful, tough, resourceful widow who stayed on the ranch, thirty miles from town, after the death of her husband, Elrick. She had been our closest neighbor, five straight-line miles from our house, but the country between us consisted of rough canyons, and the actual driving distance on gravel roads was over twenty miles.

I stepped out the back door and looked to the northwest. *There it was!* I couldn't make out flames but did see a cloud of white-and-brown smoke above the canyon rim, moving rapidly over the flat country. It had formed in the seven minutes it had taken me to return to the house. I knew it was going to be serious trouble for anyone downwind.

I rushed into the house and gave Kris the report. We weren't in the path of the fire (yet), but we needed to evacuate. Most likely the blaze would follow a path to the northeast and we could come back in the evening, after the wind died down, but Kris needed to pack an overnight bag, just in case, and we needed to get out of the canyon.

I glanced around the house. What do you take? I slipped our Mac laptops into a shoulder bag (my Mac contained all my writing files, including five unpublished Hank books), grabbed a Filson wool coat, a cap, and Kris's Nugget mandolin. She came with her overnight bag, and I told her to take a coat. It was 80 degrees outside, but March weather in our country is fickle. It might be snowing by dark.

She wondered if we should take the dogs, Dixie and our yellow Lab, Daisy. I gave that some thought. No, I didn't want to drive into town with an aromatic 90-pound Lab inside the car. I figured we would be back around dark, after the wind died down. They would be all right. We had gone through the fires of 2006 without losing a dog.

We loaded our things into Kris's Ford Explorer, drove out of our canyon to Tandy Road, and continued toward Highway 281, six miles north. When we climbed out of the Canadian River Valley and reached the flat country on top, we saw a huge cloud of dark smoke ahead of us.

In twenty minutes, the fire had travelled seven or eight miles. The caliche road and Highway 281 had disappeared inside the towering cloud, and there was no question about driving into it. We paused a moment and took a few pictures with our phones. In the minutes we were there, a line of yellow flames appeared out of the smoke.

We needed to get out of there!

TOWN

We drove back down into the valley and took a different, longer route to town, nineteen miles of dirt road to Highway 70. At that point, we would have another thirty-mile drive on pavement.

I drove as fast as I dared. My greatest fear was not the fire we had seen on the flats but rather another fire that might have started west of us, which would block our path to the highway. Up ahead, I could see streaks of white in the sky. It could have been dust or smoke from distant fires, or smoke from new fires up ahead. I couldn't tell.

We drove through the Adams ranch, the Killebrew ranch, and the Courson ranch, and didn't encounter fire. I felt great relief when we reached the highway, turned north, and headed toward Perryton and the flat farm country surrounding it. In this kind of fire situation, the best place to be was in the midst of plowed fields with no grass.

We kept a house in town and arrived there around four o'clock. It was a small duplex with no yard. Kris had used it when Mark and Ashley were in high school, on nights when driving forty miles back to the ranch wasn't handy or possible. I had never cared for the house, and in twenty years had spent only four nights there. It was just a house, not a home.

Since it appeared that we would have to spend a few hours in town, we called our friends Ken and Sandra Splawn and invited them to have supper with us. At 6, we met them at the restaurant. They hadn't heard about the fire. It seemed that nobody in town knew about it.

When I stepped out of the car, I noticed that the wind had changed. It was now coming out of the north. That was bad. A north wind could revive the fire and drive it onto our ranch.

I ordered a hamburger but hardly tasted it, and my responses to the conversation were wooden. I couldn't think of anything but the fire. During the meal, my phone rang. It was from Starla Nicholson, our neighbor who lived on the Courson ranch west of our place. She said that if we hadn't already evacuated we needed to get out, because the fire was moving south, into the Canadian River Valley.

I told her we were in town but had planned on return-
ing home after the wind died down. She said, "You can forget
that! The sheriff's department has blocked all highways and
county roads. You'd better stay in town. Dave's out with the
fire truck. This is a *bad* fire."

We went back to the town house and I realized that I
hadn't brought a travel bag—no razor, toothbrush, or hairbrush. I had nothing but the clothes I was wearing, a pair of
dusty work jeans, a faded denim work shirt, and an old pair of
shoes that were comfortable but ugly.

During the evening, Mark called several times. We
exchanged bits of information, but there wasn't much. The fire
seemed to have caught the local news media by surprise. We
received no calls from first responders on the scene, which I
interpreted as a good sign.

What news we heard sounded grim. Other fires had broken
out in in six Texas counties and parts of Oklahoma and Kansas.
The fire we had seen was being referred to as the "Perryton Fire,"
and it had rampaged east through Ochiltree, Roberts, and
Lipscomb Counties, all the way to the Oklahoma state line.

Now, with the wind shift, it had veered south, and eastern
Hemphill County was blazing. The town of Higgins had been
evacuated. Lipscomb and Canadian had been put on an evac-
uation alert. Another fire, the Lefors Fire, was threatening the
towns of Lefors and Wheeler.

A third fire, the biggest of all, had started in ranchland east
of Beaver, Oklahoma, and spread north and east into Harper
County, Oklahoma, and up into the prairie country around
Ashland, Kansas. Several towns in Oklahoma (Gate, Laverne,
and Buffalo) had been evacuated or put on high alert.

We didn't sleep well that night. A lot of people didn't sleep
well, including Mark. Here are his recollections of that night
and the following day.

MARK ERICKSON'S ACCOUNT

A friend of mine who lives in Perryton was out supplying water to one of the fire crews and he became my best source of information. He didn't know the country very well, but after he identified a few landmarks, it became clear that the fire his crew was fighting was on us. He didn't know about the house but said, "It's not looking good." At that point, I threw together an overnight bag and hit the road. I think it was around midnight.

It's about a two-hour drive to the ranch from Amarillo. I remember how peaceful the drive was: open highways beneath a clear, starry sky. On such a night, it was hard to imagine that at that moment a wildfire was ravaging the ranch and burning inside the home where I grew up.

North of Pampa, the land shifts gradually from flat farmland to rolling rangeland and then finally opens up to the Canadian River Valley. Just past Chicken Creek, there is a high spot on the highway where in daylight you can see the northern caprock way off in the distance and even make out a few landmarks on our ranch. That's where I saw the fire for the first time: a big smudge of bright orange glowing through a wall of smoke on the black canvas of night.

I continued to pester my friend with the fire crew for information. Was it headed for the house? Had it already hit the house? He wouldn't say; he just kept repeating, "It's not looking good." I've wondered since if he knew more but didn't want to be the one to deliver bad news.

When I reached the North River Road, I was surprised not to find a sheriff's deputy blocking the way. I had heard that they closed the road, but I guess by the time I got there they'd gone home for the night. About a mile in, I passed a big, military-style water truck headed out, but there didn't appear to be any other activity. I knew that there would be fire crews from all over the Panhandle scattered out across the valley fighting the fire, but I didn't see any of them.

Once I got onto the dirt roads I started to think seriously about routes in and out of the ranch. It's rough country out there, especially up in the canyons. It would be easy to drive into a trap. A route looks clear going in and the fire comes through twenty or thirty minutes later and cuts off the way out. Then you're potentially in a situation where the fire is closing in and you have to drive across country in the dark, through sandhills covered in sagebrush and plum thickets. People get killed that way.

About ten miles in, the River Road crosses Pickett Creek, a dry wash that starts in the canyon where the house is and runs down to the river. Fire was raging through the brush-covered sandhills that flank the creek bed. Flames rose over twenty feet and sent showers of cinders skyward into the breeze.

I stopped and watched. I could feel the heat from the road, and it looked like the fire was likely to cross, which could cut off the exit route. There are only two other ways out of the valley, and I had no way of knowing if they were good or not. I watched the fire burn, hoping that someone would come by who could tell me something about conditions up ahead.

A cowboy with a saddled horse in a stock trailer came through a little after 2. We talked a while and then he headed on. He was going east to another ranch and didn't know any more than I did.

I decided that was the end of the road for me that night. Any route that got me to the ranch from there was likely to be perilous. If I were going to drive in, I wasn't going to do it in the dark. I drove back to the highway, pulled over, and caught a few hours' sleep in the back seat.

I woke the next day before sunrise just as the valley was starting to get light and headed in. Smoke trails from across the north side of the valley were rising against the orangey-blue eastern horizon, some faint, some dark. They floated southward in the light northwest breeze. There was a haze over everything and pockets of smoke gathered thick in ravines and low spots. It was lovely, in a macabre sort of way.

The country was unburned through our neighbor's pasture on the west side. That gave me a little hope. Maybe the damage would be minimal. Maybe it didn't get the house. Into the west pasture and still no burned grass. But smoke was rising up ahead.

At the windmill I encountered a big burn spot where the wind-driven flames had gashed down from the north through Big Rocks Canyon and hugged the bottom of a hill heading east into a pass between the caprock and a large mesa. That pass is the only way from the west pasture to Pickett Canyon where the house is located. It runs nearly a mile through a tight, brushy corridor with rough country and caprocks on both sides.

In other words, just one way out and a lot of stuff to burn. I could see smoke rising out of it as the pickup tilted upward into the pass. My pulse began to rise and I pressed the accelerator. If I was going to make a dash, best dash fast.

The fire had skirted the caprock going east into the pass so that the burned areas were only on my left. At the top of the pass there was live fire and smoldering skeletons of trees on both sides of the road. There was no distinct fire line, just scattered fire and burned spots on all sides.

When I got through the corridor and the land opened up a bit, I headed north into Pickett Canyon. At the crossroads is an old wooden barn. It was standing, unburned. A couple hundred yards further up the road was the bunkhouse. It was gone, leveled; just a smoking blank spot.

I kept going. The house was a mile further into the canyon. About halfway there, the road turns and the house comes into view for a moment. That morning I couldn't see it. There was a lot of fire in the canyon. If the house was standing, it was obscured by smoke in the dim, pre-dawn half-light.

On across the dam and through the trees, and then I was there, pulling up into the driveway. One of my parents' dogs, Daisy, was standing in the driveway barking, as she did every time someone *drove up to the house. Only this time, there was no house behind her, just a grand, smoldering ruin, the rock chimney the only object rising above the debris.*

I got out and looked around. It was quiet and oddly peaceful. Fire calmly crackled in the wreckage, in the half-burned trees in the yard, in the cedar-post yard fence. There was no sign of the other dog, Dixie.

I'm not sure how long I was there just looking around at the wreckage, but eventually I loaded Daisy, covered in soot, into the back seat of the pickup and went to check on the rest of the ranch. I called my dad as soon as I had a cell phone signal. He was with my mother, who was listening on speaker phone.

There's no way to soften some news, so you just have to spill it. That's how this was. No poetry or nuance, just the blunt truth: "The house is gone."

TUESDAY, MARCH 7

Kris and I were up at daylight and anxious to go home. We packed our things and drove to McDonald's for breakfast. As we were about to get out of the car, I got a call from Mark.

He hadn't been able to sleep and had left Amarillo to check on the ranch. The valley was still on fire when he got there, so he slept in his pickup until daylight. He was able to drive through the blackened, smoking valley, and reached our home.

He said, "Mom, Dad, I have terrible news. The house is gone."

Kris let out a cry. I swallowed hard. "The bunkhouse?"

"Gone."

"My writing office?"

"I haven't looked, but it couldn't have survived."

Kris moaned and I sat in stunned silence. We had lost *everything*. It would take us months to comprehend what that meant.

We went inside the restaurant and ordered breakfast and coffee, then drove downtown to the Radio Shack. We had left the ranch in such haste, I had neglected to bring charging cables for our cell phones and the battery on mine was getting low—at a very critical time, since I was already getting calls and text messages from friends and relatives who wondered if we were all right, or even alive.

I told callers that we had survived but were now homeless.

When we walked into Radio Shack, several of the employees gave us long looks. They had already heard. News travels fast in small towns. We are tied together in many ways.

I told an employee, George Macias, that I needed a power cord and he found one. I looked toward the rear of the store and saw Kerry Symons, the owner, coming toward us at a brisk walk. He and his wife Cynthia attended our church and sang with us in the choir.

In the early '60s, Kerry and I lived on the same block in Perryton. He was a toddler, I a senior in high school. After graduation, we both went out to find a bigger world, then ended up back in Perryton. He now owned fourteen Radio Shack stores and sat on the company's board. He was an important man but few people knew it, because he never told anyone.

His head was down and he wore a grave expression. He hugged Kris, put an arm around me, and blinked back tears. "I'm so sorry."

I told him that I didn't know if my office had survived the fire. If not, I would be back to replace my Verizon modem so that I could connect with the internet. Kerry told George, "Get him set up with another modem."

That was a good decision by Kerry.

THE LONG RIDE "HOME"

Kris and I began the long, silent, forty-mile drive to whatever was left of our ranch. Twenty-one miles south of town, we turned east on Highway 281. We had gone about three miles when we began seeing the black scar off to the south, a line that was pointing to the northeast.

At mile 5, we saw what the fire had left of a two-mile shelter belt of trees that had been planted during the Depression, probably by workers in the Civilian Conservation Corps. Those sturdy cedars and ash trees had survived the droughts of the '30s and '50s, as well as the drought of 2011–2014. They had survived at least two fires that I knew about and a tornado in 2009.

Now we saw them blackened, twisted, broken, and smoldering. The utility poles around them were on fire and some had burned in half. The asphalt pavement beside the tree row had been altered by the heat.

Those trees must have been the source of the cloud of dark smoke we had seen the day before. Burning grass produces smoke that is mostly white. Black smoke is a sign of burning cedar trees, which contain an oily sap that burns like petroleum.

At the end of the tree row, we turned south on County Road 23. Had we continued driving east, we would have passed the Githens' place, the house and barns destroyed. Beyond the Githens' home, a big metal hog barn had collapsed onto itself.

We drove south on CR 23. Off to the left, we saw what remained of Tark Cook's section of Old World Bluestem grass that, the day before, had stood eighteen inches tall and made waves in the wind. What remained was 640 acres of black desert. We saw the same on the west side of the road, and to the south, as far as we could see, nothing but ash and dirt.

A mile beyond the tree row, we came to three utility poles that had burned in half and were still flaming. The wires had not broken but the burning poles blocked half the road, so I had to drive in the ditch to continue.

Two miles beyond the tree row, where the road took a sharp turn to the left, I caught a glimpse of Betsy Brownlee's house off to the west, now a pile of smoking rubble. She had grown up on the place and after a career as a school librarian had retired, moved back to the ranch, and built a house.

It was directly in the path of the fire and she knew nothing about the impending danger. She was in the kitchen, baking cookies when Mike Wheat, our game warden, drove to the house, told her to evacuate, and saved her life. She escaped but lost everything.

Another two miles brought us to the caprock that gave a broad view of the Canadian River Valley. In better times, that spot had always stirred my heart, capturing the wild grandeur of this marvelous piece of the world. It wasn't a stirring sight today, just mile after mile of cinders and the skeletons of burned mesquites and cedars. From that spot, I could see our east pasture, mostly black and still burning.

We drove off the caprock and continued through the Adams ranch to the cattle guard that led onto our property. There, we saw fire trucks in the distance, fighting flames west of the road. We still had fire on the ranch, but I didn't see it as a threat to us. The wind had calmed and there wasn't much left to burn, just a few islands of grass. The canyons and mesas would continue to burn for days.

We drove north through smoke and came to the barn. It hadn't been touched by the fire, due to the fact that the area around it had been denuded by vehicle traffic. I was glad to see that my Caterpillar skid-steer tractor, a sixty-thousand-dollar piece of equipment, had survived. In weeks to come, we would use it for loading and unloading hundreds of round bales of hay.

I looked off to the northeast, toward the stack lot, and was relieved to see that sixteen round bales of alfalfa had survived. We would need them. Our cattle had no grass to eat . . . if we had any cattle left. News reports on the radio were full of horrible stories about ranchers who had lost 30 to 50 percent of their cow herds. Early estimates of death loss ranged between 2,000 and 3,000.

We continued north, past the shipping pens. We slowed and glanced off to the west at a heap of rubble: the bunkhouse. When we bought the ranch in 1990, it had been the only structure on the place, a 20' x 30' two-bedroom camp shack with a big gas heating stove and no air conditioning. The water froze up every winter and the house was a haven for mice, packrats, snakes, bats, coons, and skunks. Even so, I used it as my office for fifteen years and wrote a number of Hank books there.

In 2008, we moved the old house two hundred yards north to a better location, and our son-in-law spent the summer rebuilding it into a snug little lodge for family and guests: clean, bright, comfortable, and free of vermin. It wasn't big or fancy, just cozy.

Only three days before, George Clay and Jeff Nichols, friends from downstate, had spent the night there and had watched the sunrise from the front porch. Now there was no porch and no bunkhouse. Nothing.

THE HOUSE

We continued north into Pickett Canyon and followed the road across the dam. Cedar trees and railroad ties were still burning in many places.

The day of the fire, I had parked my one-ton Chevy pickup and the Polaris Ranger in the circle drive in front of the house.

It had seemed as safe a place to leave them as any, and sure enough, both vehicles survived. On the left side of the pickup, the side facing the house, some of the rubber and plastic had melted, and neither window on that side would roll down, but otherwise the pickup had come through in good shape. If the tires had ignited, we would have lost both vehicles.

The big oak tree Kris had started from a Walmart sprig in 1993 was now a tortured skeleton. Most of the piñon pines we had brought in from Wagon Mound, New Mexico, had suffered the same fate.

We stopped in front of what remained of our beautiful log home. It was all gone except the ghost of a stone chimney. Kris uttered a moan and we stared in silence. She told me later, "I didn't have any tears. I couldn't cry."

We got out of the car and walked up the flagstone steps that Bill Dudley and I, dripping sweat in the 105-degree heat, had built in the summer of 1994. The house rubble was still hot and smoking, and we recognized a few charred items: an exercise bike, porch chairs, hot-water heaters, the Viking stove, the deep freeze and refrigerator, washer and dryer. Everything else, the accumulation of twenty-four years, was ash.

Where we lived, electric power came through miles of lines that were vulnerable to storms, and a reliable generator was an important piece of equipment. In 2014, I had spent a lot of money to buy the best one available, and it had served us well during the sixteen-day power outage in January.

I could see that our 45kW generator, north of the house, had become a blackened hunk and appeared to be a total loss. Its John Deere industrial engine had retained its green paint, but two of the four tires, the battery, battery case, control panel, and all the wiring had burned or melted.

The fireplace remained intact, although part of the chimney had fallen. In summer 1993, Gilbert Harper, a gifted brick mason, had spent weeks building it with stones Mark, Ashley, and I gathered on the ranch. I recalled watching Gilbert and his assistant picking through the pile of stones, inspecting each and choosing the one that was just right for the spot. That profession required a kind of patience unknown to me.

Gilbert did splendid work, and we had enjoyed many a long winter evening in front of that fireplace. After an ice storm in 2009, it heated our house for nine days.

WIND SONG

Just then, Mark drove up in his red Chevy pickup. Daisy, our yellow Lab, jumped out and came loping over to greet us, as she had always done when we returned from town, telling us with a swinging tail and a happy face, "Welcome home!" It was a sad ritual now.

Dixie, the heeler and Daisy's constant companion, didn't appear. We hoped she might be hiding somewhere and would show up later.

Mark had been out looking at the pastures and checking the cattle. He had spent his childhood in this place and had grown into a big, handsome man, wearing an old felt cowboy hat. He hugged his mother, then me. We stood in silence, our thoughts flying over those twenty-four years we had spent in the house.

It was the house of Mark's childhood, the house where Kris had homeschooled Mark and Ashley, cooked thousands of meals in her spacious kitchen, made wild plum jelly and salsa from garden vegetables, sewed quilts, and presided over a big family feast every Thanksgiving.

Mark interrupted my thoughts. "I think the cattle might be okay. I got a pretty good count and didn't see any with burns. Wind Song is missing."

Wind Song was a gray Arabian mare, thirty-three years old and one of six horses in the upper west pasture. At one time she had been my number-one using horse. I had thrown my saddle on her back many a dark morning, and we had covered many a mile together in the Canadian River Valley.

She had served me well for more than twenty years, with the exception of one day in August, 2006. We were gathering cattle on the south side of the river, jogging down a small hill. She dropped her head to grab a bite of green grass, lost her footing, and did a cartwheel, slamming me into the ground. I broke several ribs, but at least she didn't run off and leave me afoot.

During the winter of 2016–2017, she had been showing her age and had gotten thin. Most likely she wasn't able to outrun the fire and got trapped. Several days later, Mark and Nathan Dahlstrom found her body.

THE CATTLE

I could hardly believe that we hadn't lost any cattle, and it seemed almost beyond belief that they had come through such a conflagration without being maimed in some way. I thought about that many times in the weeks to follow and concluded that a combination of factors had spared them.

First, they were not in the path of the fire in its early stages, the period between 2:30 and 5:30, when it was being driven by a dry southwest wind that gusted to seventy miles an hour. Cattle couldn't outrun such a fire, and in the flat pastures north and east of our place, they had no place to hide.

Second, when the wind shifted to the north around 5:30, the fire changed directions, moving south into our country below the caprock, but the north wind lacked some of the punch of the southwest wind. Our cattle had more time to move around and find safe spots.

Third, they were located in pastures below the caprock, rugged country that might have slowed the wind and offered some protection in low spots. Also, the caprock regions had thin soil and grew less grass than the better country to the north. Less grass—and shorter grass—meant less fuel.

Whatever reasons we might come up with, we can't overlook another factor: the cattle that survived the fire were *smart*. I have spent a lifetime around bovines and have done my share of cussing them and calling them stupid, but in the face of a killer fire, they had made intelligent decisions: moving away from the flames, taking refuge in low spots and bare spots, and shifting to places where the fire had already destroyed the fuel. That is a form of intelligence you have to respect.

Mark's report turned out to be mostly correct. We lost one yearling but no cows or calves. In fact, two calves were born while the ranch was still burning.

The cows had survived, but they had lost about 90 percent of their pasture. Before the fire, feeding on this place had been a pretty leisurely affair, about right for a 73-year-old writer who was drifting toward laziness. Six days a week, I drove my pickup or, if the weather wasn't too cold, the open-cab Ranger, to four pastures and poured out sacked feed to cows in two pastures, yearlings in another, and horses in another.

I didn't have to feed hay because our ranch had an abundance of grass left over from the summer growing season. Most of that grass was gone now, and feeding would be different. We would have to feed every day, double the amount of protein, and put out round bales of hay as well as feed pellets. I had sixteen round bales of alfalfa, but they wouldn't last long.

Mark and I had cattle to feed and Kris drove back to town. I could only imagine the thoughts she carried.

PHONE CALLS

Mark and I split up, headed in different directions, and started feeding pastures that were still burning. Mark fed cake and I delivered round bales with the track loader. All the while, our phones were buzzing with text messages and phone calls from people in Perryton, Canadian, Miami, and Amarillo, saying, "Our prayers are with you. What do you need? Just let us know."

What did we need? We had no idea. It would take weeks for us to sort that out. To be honest, I didn't want to talk to anyone. I didn't know how I was doing or what we needed or what I was supposed to say. I was cold and weary and everything had become a blur.

Noon Vela, a farmer-rancher and longtime friend, was one of the first callers. "I've got hay, equipment, labor, whatever you need. Just let me know." A woman in Austin, whose name I didn't recognize, said she and her husband would be at the ranch the next day with two truckloads of hay.

Friends in Amarillo, Bowie, and Canyon made similar assurances. If I had accepted all the offers of hay, we might have had five thousand round bales on the ranch. I told them to hold off for a few days.

One of the text messages came from Nathan Dahlstrom, a friend in Lubbock who always came to the ranch to help us brand and wean. "I'll be there tomorrow, whether you want me or not."

Another set of texts came from Nikki Georgacakis in San Antonio. She worked for Maverick Books, edited and designed the Hank books, and managed our Hank website and social media. She had been a guest in our home many times, and now she wanted to make the eleven-hour drive to the Panhandle to help. She seemed determined to come.

When I got back to town that night, three ladies from the church knocked on the door. Mary Dudley had heard that I had lost all my clothes and brought jeans and work shirts that had belonged to her late husband, Bill Dudley. He had died two years before after a long battle with leukemia, and Mary had kept his clothes in a closet.

Bill and I had hunted deer and birds on the ranch, and he had served as cook at several of our roundups. Their son Chris had been one of Mark's best friends growing up.

Mary said, "I can't think of a better use for Bill's clothes than to give them to you." We hugged. She couldn't have given me a better gift, because I didn't own a stitch of clothes except the faded jeans and denim shirt I was wearing, and they reeked of smoke.

She handed me six pairs of jeans and six shirts. For the next two weeks, that was my wardrobe, and I was still wearing them months later. The shirts fit well (Bill had been tall and long-armed), but the jeans were a bit snug in the waist. I had to suck in and tug to get the button in the hole.

I don't remember what we ate for supper that night, but someone from the church had brought food. The church ladies had gotten together and were watching over us like angels.

WEDNESDAY, MARCH 8

Around 9 in the morning, our pastor, Mark Metzger, arrived at the town house to express his sympathy. He came inside and we talked for a while, then we joined hands as he prayed for us and for others in the area who had suffered death and destruction.

From there, I went to the bank. I had lost all my checkbooks, banking records, and fifteen years of receipts for the IRS. I ordered new checks from Veronica Herrera. It happened that her husband, Juan Carlos, tended some wells on our ranch for Apache Petroleum, a nice fellow. Veronica fixed me up.

I picked up a breakfast burrito and some beef jerky at a convenience store. On my way out, I noticed a stack of Amarillo newspapers with the big headline, "Taken in Their Prime." The entire front page was devoted to stories and photographs about the fires of March 6. I bought a copy and slipped it into my shoulder bag, which had become my portable office and filing cabinet.

I had been so preoccupied with my own problems that I'd given little thought to the tragedies that had occurred to the east and south of us: the death of Cade Koch, age 22, in Lipscomb County, and the deaths of Cody Crockett, Sydney Wallace, and Sloan Everett on the Franklin ranch in Gray County.

Koch had left from work at the lumber yard in Canadian and was on his way to Lipscomb to check on his pregnant wife when he was trapped by the fire and died of smoke inhalation. The other three, all young, bright, beautiful kids in their prime, were trying to save cattle from the Lefors fire. Cody and Sydney were engaged to be married. Sloan left a wife and two small children.

The following August, in the cover story of *Texas Monthly*, veteran writer Skip Hollandsworth reconstructed events of the afternoon of March 6. Cody, Sydney, and Sloan were on the Franklin ranch, moving a group of heifers out of the path of the fire. They must have thought they were safe. Then, around 6, the wind shifted to the northwest and drove the flames over them, moving so fast they couldn't escape on horses and a four-wheeler.

That was the same change in wind direction I had noticed outside the restaurant in Perryton at six o'clock Monday evening, and the one that sent the fire down into our canyon. Those wind shifts are very common in March and are the primary cause of death in wildfires. You think the fire is predictable, but it's not.

Hollandsworth effectively described the destruction of the fires and captured the staggering loss experienced by the families and communities of those young people. I didn't know any of them personally but started first grade with Cade Koch's grandfather, Curt Warren, and had worked cattle with Cody Crockett's grandfather, Bobby Thompson.

From the convenience store, I headed south to the ranch. One of our local radio stations, KXDJ, ran a four-hour morning talk show that did a good job of covering local news, which now included nonstop coverage of the fire. We were just beginning to understand the magnitude of the destruction in Texas, Oklahoma, and Kansas.

Our fire, the Perryton fire, was only one of thirty-two wildfires reported that day, a level of intensity unprecedented in modern history. (www.southernclimate.org/documents/Wildfire_Report. pdf). The damage was widespread and enormous.

East Lefors fire: 92,571 acres.

Starbuck fire: 662,687 acres.

Perryton fire: 318,056 acres.

Over 1.2 million total acres burned.

Eighty-seven structures and 1,500 miles of fencing destroyed.

Seven people dead, five injured.

Livestock deaths between 9,000 and 10,000.

This was the largest fire outbreak in modern history, surpassing the 2006 total of 1.1 million acres burned. The Perryton fire was the third largest in Texas history. The Starbuck fire was the largest wildfire in Kansas history.

Christopher Samples, who hosted the KXDJ morning show, recognized the fire to be what it was: a disaster for rural residents and ranchers in three states. But he reported that help was pouring in from all directions, in the form of fencing material, food, bottled water, sacked feed, and semi-loads of hay coming from South Texas, Colorado, South Dakota, and even Michigan. In our area, goods were being stockpiled at drop-off points in Canadian, Pampa, Wheeler, and Lipscomb.

Leaving town, I could see smoke on the southern horizon and knew that the fires were still burning in the Canadian River Valley, and probably on our ranch. Sure enough, at the cattle guard going into our place, I saw active fire in the mesa pasture and clouds of smoke to the west. In the distance, a small fire truck was spraying water on a line of fire.

Several vehicles were parked near the cattle guard. I stopped and exchanged words with Ochiltree County Deputies Floyd and Herrington. They had spent the past two days with the fire, catching naps in their pickups.

Daisy was waiting at the barn and came bounding out to greet me. She had lost her home and had taken up residence in the barn. Mark was there too, and a bit later, Nathan Dahlstrom arrived from Lubbock. Nathan and his family had been our close friends for years. He wanted to see the ruins of the house, so we drove up into Pickett Canyon and walked around. He was close to tears. "Boss,'" he said, "I'm sorry."

THE ASHES

I had no desire to walk through the ruins. The destruction appeared to be total and I felt numb. When Mark had said those words on the phone Tuesday morning—"The house is gone"—a curtain dropped on that period of my life. Everything was gone and that was the end of it. It didn't occur to me that there might be anything worth saving.

But Mark wanted to look around. He went to the spot that had once been a closet by the front door, where we had kept our coats, boots, and hats. I had lost all my boots, cowboy hats, wool vests, winter caps, warm gloves, and an Eddie Bauer goose-down parka that was very effective against wind-driven cold.

Mark began digging around in the ash with a stick. He found something and held it up. "Look what I found!" It was one of his spurs with his name on the heel band. Nathan cheered.

Those spurs were a gift from me when Mark was about fifteen and had proved himself a good cowboy. He had "earned his spurs." He chose a well-respected spur maker in Amarillo named Cates and put the spurs to good use over the years.

Mark was always a good cowboy, naturally gifted and quick to learn. On the river, he'd ridden big country with some good teachers: Jim Streeter, Jack White, Jim Nicholson, Jason Pelham, Burk Adcock, Dave Nicholson, Billy DeArmond, and Jody Chisum. And me. Maybe he'd learned something from his old man.

He and Nathan dug some more in the ashes, and Nathan pulled out one of my spurs with "Hank" on the heel band. I had ordered them from R. F. Ford of Water Valley, Texas, in the early 1990s at the Cowboy Symposium in Lubbock. They had been my first and only pair of custom-made spurs and I had gone many a mile with them over the years.

The boys continued stirring the rubble and came up with the other two spurs, as well as the buckles from Mark's spur straps. We walked around for a while, remembering better times. I thought of a photograph someone had taken of Nathan sitting in a big chair in front of the fireplace, reading to a lapful of children, his two daughters and small son.

As we walked back toward the pickup, Nathan heard something stirring in a shrub. He thought it might be Dixie, the blue heeler that had gone missing. He and Mark searched the shrub but didn't find the dog. It must have been a bird.

Dixie never showed up, and we must assume that she died in the fire. It's hard to imagine how that happened. There were places south of the house that didn't burn, two dry ponds that would have been safe havens. Daisy, the big happy Lab, survived without any sign of damage.

Dixie was a smart dog but had a morbid fear of loud noises. A gunshot, bullwhip, or clap of thunder would send her streaking to a safe corner of the porch. I imagine that's where she was when the fire hit. Even a smart dog doesn't expect the porch to collapse on top of her.

The 70th Hank book, *The Case of the Troublesome Lady*, contains a scene where Hank is trying to impress Miss Scamper and performs a difficult trick that he calls Food Bowl Parade, pushing a dog food bowl around in circles with his nose. I borrowed that stunt from Dixie. In her prime, she was able to flip the bowl in the air with her nose and catch it in her mouth.

FEEDING CATTLE

It was time to start feeding cattle, a routine that we would be following until green grass returned or until we moved the cattle to another location. They had nothing to eat in the pastures. Every bite of nutrition would have to come from us. Mark and Nathan loaded the flatbed pickup with hay and cake and went east. I got into the tractor and hauled round bales to the west pasture.

The east face of Hodges Mesa, visible from the barn, was in flames, and cedar trees exploded in puffs of black smoke. The terrain was too rough for fire trucks, and much of the grassland around it had already burned, so it wasn't much of a threat. It would just have to burn itself out. A column of smoke rose from the west side of the mesa, indicating that we still had fires in the west pasture and on the ranches that joined us. They burned all day.

When I got back to the barn, Kam Dodson and Phil Symons pulled up with a trailer-load of hay: sixteen round bales. They dumped out the bales and I used the tractor to move them into a grass trap we were using as a stack lot. Most of the grass in the trap had burned, so we considered it safe, even though we still had live fires in the area.

Mark told Kam of another problem we faced: we had lost electricity to the ranch. Many of the utility poles were on the ground and still burning. We had lost the use of five submersible pumps in three pastures, and we needed stock water. Kam drove back to Perryton, hooked onto a trailer with a 700-gallon tank, and spent the day delivering water to our cattle and horses. We appreciated his help but knew it was only a temporary solution.

Nathan had come with a cooler of sandwich material, burritos and salsa, and bottled water. We ate a picnic lunch in front of the "house," then went back to the feeding.

Another trailer-load of hay arrived in the afternoon, delivered by a man I had never met, J. B. Ham of Amarillo. He was a friend of our son Scot and had made the four-hour round trip to bring sixteen bales of good triticale hay. When he got back to Amarillo, he loaded up another sixteen bales and delivered them to the ranch after we had gone back to town. He unloaded the bales himself in the dark, using the tractor. He devoted the entire day to helping us.

At some point during the day, Doug Wilkens showed up at the ranch. Doug was a friend of many years, had worked on the ranch as a cowboy and archeologist, and loved the place as much as anyone. He asked what he could do to help and I told him that, with Mark and Nathan around, we had everything fairly well under control.

And, let's be honest, I didn't want to ask anyone for help. Call it pride or stubbornness.

One of our tasks for the afternoon was to move five horses from the upper west pasture to the shipping pens. The flat country on top had taken close to a 100 percent loss in the fire. The horses had nothing to eat, and I was pretty sure that breathing ash wouldn't be good for them. Further, the only source of water, an electric submersible pump, had lost power, due to the fact that there were twenty burned poles between us and the main line on Highway 281.

Nathan and I drove up the long, steep hill that led from the valley floor to the upper west. I was surprised to see that the cows from the west pasture had migrated up to the top country in the upper west. There was no fence between the two pastures, only a canyon wall that rose somewhere between 250 and 300 feet. Moving from one pasture to the other had required cunning and an expenditure of energy. No doubt the cows had found a deer trail and hiked up the caprock.

The horses came to us at a gallop, so we opened the gate on the south end and led them down the long hill into the valley. Once they reached the bottom, they knew the routine and ran a mile east and north to the pens, where they knew they would get half a sack of feed. We kept them overnight in the pens, where they were safe from fire, and gave them a round bale of grass hay.

Mark, Nathan, and I discussed what to do with the cattle in the upper west. The pasture had no grass and no electric pump for water. Mark thought he knew where they had climbed out of the west: a deer trail on the north end that followed a finger of Big Rocks Canyon. He thought he might be able to coax them down the trail with some feed. Nathan and Mark went back on top to try that, while I put out more round bales with the tractor.

Around sundown, the boys returned. They had worn themselves out putting out feed along the deer trail and climbing in and out of Big Rocks Canyon, but the plan hadn't worked. The cows wanted to stay in the top country. We loaded feed and drove back up the caprock and fed them. They came to the sound of the pickup horn, but not at their usual pace. They were moving very slowly, slower than I had ever seen them move. They must have been exhausted.

The good news, though, was that we didn't see any signs of burned hair, damaged hooves, or blindness on the cattle. That was amazing. We had heard reports on the radio about thousands of cattle in Lipscomb and Hemphill Counties, east of us, that had been killed, maimed, and blinded by the fire. Our neighbors to the east were having to endure a kind of torment that we were spared: doctoring burned animals or shooting them to put them out of their misery.

You can call that "euthanizing" or "putting them down," but it means that ranchers were killing animals they had raised and fed and cared for. Many of those tough cow people couldn't talk about it without crying.

At the end of the afternoon, all the animals on our ranch had hay, feed, and water. We had stopped the bleeding. Before the fire had changed our lives, Mark had planned to drive to Austin on Wednesday. A friend of ours, movie director/writer Jeff Nichols, was going to be inducted into the Texas Film Hall of Fame on Thursday night, and Mark had been invited to sit at the Nichols table.

The fire had put those plans in limbo, but I urged him to go. We had stabilized things at the ranch and Nathan planned to stay another day, so Mark might as well go to Austin and help Jeff celebrate this great honor. (Jeff had visited the ranch three days before the fire and was the last person to spend the night in the bunkhouse.)

Mark drove back to Amarillo to prepare for his trip, and Nathan spent the night with us in town. I was dog-tired. Nathan was younger and stronger than I but had worked twice as hard, hiking up and down the canyon walls, and he too was worn out. While Nikki warmed up a meal that had been brought by the church ladies, Nathan stretched out on the couch and slept.

After supper, I seized the opportunity to take a bath. After spending the day on a burned-out ranch, I reeked of smoke, as did the inside of my pickup, my wool coat, everything. My bath water acquired the color of dust and cinders.

I fell right to sleep but woke up around 2:30. Kris was awake, too, and we talked for an hour. I suppose you would say that we were grieving. During the day, we had tried to put on a brave face for friends who were concerned about us, but now, alone and together, we grieved.

Kris's home had been the center of her life. She had given it her love and creativity. It had expressed the beauty of her soul and contained the items she wanted to pass on to the next generation. It was hard to let it go.

THURSDAY, MARCH 9

When Nathan and I made it to the ranch that morning, we could see fire trucks working several lines of fire still burning in the mesa pasture, and a column of gray-black smoke was rising behind the mesa, in the west pasture. A white one-ton dually flatbed pickup approached. It was one of two fire rigs from Harold Courson's C Bar C ranch, and I recognized the three men wearing firefighter gear: Jody Chisum, Dave Nicholson, and Trevor Chisum.

There was no telling how long they had gone without sleep. They expressed their sadness at the loss of our house and I thanked them for their efforts. Seeing them brought back memories of the fires of 2006, the night the fire jumped the river and was burning across the Adams ranch. I had been trying to extinguish burning mesquite stumps with my tractor around midnight when I encountered the C Bar C crew on the county road.

Now, with Mark gone, I swallowed my pride and called Doug Wilkens. Yes, I needed help. Also, did he have a warm vest? The weather had turned cold and I had lost all my vests in the fire.

At the barn, Doug, Nathan, and I split up the workload. All the stock had to be fed hay and cake, and I had to unload another trailer-load of hay that had just arrived from . . . I don't remember whom. Some kind soul from somewhere showed up, unannounced, with a flatbed trailer loaded with prairie hay.

Up to this point, I hadn't looked for our three bulls in Pickett Canyon and assumed they had died. That canyon had not burned in the twenty-seven years we had owned the ranch, and it was loaded with cedar trees. When the fire came down into the canyon Monday night, it must have burned like a lumber yard.

I couldn't imagine that the bulls had survived, especially when you consider that a canyon holds heat like a fire pit. But when I drove north into Pickett Canyon, expecting to find smoking carcasses of three registered Bonsmara bulls, I was amazed to find them standing on an unburned flat of ground where we parked our stock trailers. They were hungry and ready for feed and came at a fast walk. One of them had a watery eye, but other than that they appeared to be unburned and undamaged.

How that happened, where they went to escape death or injury in that burning canyon, I will never know.

While Wilkens fed the east side of the ranch, Nathan and I drove over to the west pasture. At the windmill, the fires were so close we could hear the crackle of the flames, but the wind wasn't blowing so we weren't in any danger. It created an eerie scene: our cattle eating feed cubes beside flames that were still eating our ranch.

Off in the distance, we could see fire trucks spraying a line of fire and a big John Deere dozer plowing a fire guard. Overhead, a twin-engine airplane circled the area several times. I was told it contained officials from the Texas Forest Service, checking the location of the fires and radioing instructions to crews on the ground. They wanted to get this fire killed dead, before the wind picked up and sent it raging in another direction.

SCOT

When we got back to the barn, I saw a white semi-truck with a Caterpillar D6 dozer on the flatbed trailer. Scot Erickson, our older son, was undoing chains. We met and hugged. "I'm sorry, Dad." He looked away and blinked, then got straight to the business.

"I'll be back tomorrow with a backhoe and skid-steer tractor. People have been calling and texting me for two days, asking what they can do. I'll have twenty-five people and two dump trucks here on Saturday. We'll get this place cleaned up. Calico County is catering the lunch. Love you guys, bye."

And off he went in a roar of diesel smoke and a cloud of caliche dust. What a kid. While the rest of us were still stunned and walking around like zombies, he had taken charge of the cleanup. It was time to start over and rebuild.

This must have been around five o'clock, and Nathan had to drive back to Lubbock. He wanted to stay, and I wished that he could stay, but he had other commitments he had to honor.

Scot checked in with me several times that day. In one of our conversations I suggested that we needed a camper trailer to give us a place to rest, eat lunch, and use the bathroom, and a place where Mark could spend the night when he came back from Austin.

Late in the afternoon, Wilkens and I had finished feeding when Scot called again. "Got a camper trailer to rent. Dan O'Quinn is on his way with it. Meet him at North River Road and lead him in. Have him check your pickup and make sure the fire didn't burn the brake lines. You could get yourself killed."

THE CAMPER

Wilkens and I got into my pickup and made the nineteen-mile drive to the spot, north of the Canadian River Bridge, where Highway 70 intersected with North River Road. On the way, Scot called again. "Dan's going to be late. He had a blowout, but he's back on the road."

We reached Highway 70 and waited. Scot called again. "Dan had another blowout, but he thinks he can make it to River Road. I called Jim's Tire Service and they're sending a man out with four new tires. Dad, I'm sorry. I know you're tired."

Yes, I was tired, but so was everyone else in our burned-out world. Wilkens and I waited. Around 6:45, we saw Dan's white dually pickup creeping toward us on the shoulder, pulling a large camper trailer. He crossed the cattle guard and parked on the side of the caliche road.

Dan was one of Scot's oldest and most loyal friends. They had helped each other through some bad times, and now Dan had accepted the job of delivering a camper trailer to a ranch out in the Wild West, enduring two blowouts on the way. He owned and managed Texas Body Shop in Amarillo, having taken it over from his father. He had grown up in the business and was an astute observer of all things mechanical. He could fix anything.

He was embarrassed about the tires. "I checked them and they looked okay, but tires go bad when they sit for a few years. These were just waiting to fall apart. I guess we'll all be late for supper."

That drew a laugh. I asked Dan to check the brake lines on my pickup, which he did with a flashlight, and said everything looked okay.

After a bit, we saw a pickup turn onto North River Road. It was Felix Rosales from Jim's Tire Service. Instead of enjoying a quiet supper with his wife after a hard day of fixing flats, he had been called out to replace four trailer tires on a cold, dark night in the middle of a dirt road in Roberts County. His easy smile and pleasant manner suggested that it was no big deal.

It was a big deal to me and would have been for any other human being I had ever known.

We held flashlights and watched him break the bead on four tubeless tires, using a big hammer that he swung above his head and delivered to the place where the rim met the bead of the tire. It was a small target. The hammer had to hit the right spot, and he never missed. Then we watched him fit each new tire on the rim, using only hand tools, liquid soap, and his knees to force the tire over the rim.

When he let down the air jack and put away his tools, I draped my arm around his thick shoulder and thanked him for coming. "I hope your kids are proud of what you do. They should be. You're a hero to me."

We made our way back to the ranch and parked the trailer near the spot where the bunkhouse had stood. It had an RV hookup for water and electricity—which would be welcome when the North Plains Electric crews got the power lines repaired. Dan headed back to Amarillo and Wilkens and I drove to Perryton in the dark.

I dragged myself into the town house around ten o'clock. Once again, ladies from the church had brought supper. Nikki served it up and reported on her day. She had filled out applications for replacement titles for four vehicles and two stock trailers, shopped for groceries and household items, and purchased an office computer and printer to replace the ones I had lost in the fire.

I took a bath and washed off the day's soot and dust. Again, the water was an ugly shade of brown when I was done.

FRIDAY, MARCH 10

One of the things that was shattered by the fire was my daily routine of rising early, going to my office, and writing until ten o'clock. It was a pattern I established shortly after Kris and I got married in 1967, and I had maintained it in a rather fanatical way for five decades. Under that stern regime, I had written a lot of books and magazine articles.

Now, living in a little duplex in town, everything had changed. I needed to restart the routine, so I began going to the Maverick Books warehouse in the early morning hours and using Gary Rinker's office and desk. It wasn't my usual place, and I couldn't hear the coyotes howling, but it was warm and dry, with electric lights and inside plumbing, and I was glad to have it.

I was there Friday morning, writing notes about the fire, when Doug Wilkens showed up with some clothes: a warm vest, a brush jacket, and some loose-fitting warm-ups for eveningwear. He had brought a pair of his dress boots, but they were too small for me.

Later, Wilkens and I met down at the ranch and split up the feeding chores. There were still some fires burning in the canyons on the Killebrew ranch, west of us, but the fires on our property had finally died out. I hauled round bales with the tractor to the cattle in the west and mesa pastures, while Wilkens drove to the east pasture with cake and two round bales, one on the pickup's flatbed and the other on a two-wheel bale trailer.

The cows that had drifted from the west to the upper west were still there, in the same spot where we had fed them the day before. I wanted to move them back down to the west. Not only was the upper west a desert of ash and cinders, but we still had no electricity to the submersible pump, and water had become a problem. Crews from the electric company were working to replace burned poles and fix broken lines, but we had no idea how long that would take.

Two more trailer-loads of grass hay showed up that morning. The drivers had come 640 miles from Floresville, Texas, and I never figured out how they found me. It might have been more of Scot's work. He had wide connections and loyal friends.

I had to unload the hay with the tractor and told Wilkens to see if he could call the cows in the upper west down the long hill into the valley, then get them into the west pasture. He tried but didn't feel right about it. The cows were still lethargic, moving slowly, and he was afraid the cows might follow him down the hill, leaving some of the baby calves on top. He fed them cake where we'd fed them the day before and left them there.

I knew he'd made the right call on that. When you move cows with small calves, you have to be careful that you don't separate the calves from their mothers. Cows have astonishing instincts when it comes to motherhood, and most of the time they're able to correct the bad decisions we make in the name of "ranch management," but we should try not to make their job too difficult.

SCOT AND TINA

In the afternoon, Scot arrived with his semi, this time carrying a backhoe and skid-steer tractor. His wife, Tina, was riding in the cab with him. I was glad to see her. She had a bright smile and a reservoir of quiet strength we needed in such a sad time, and she was always ready to pitch in and help, regardless of the task.

Scot bailed out of the cab of the truck and began rattling off orders. He'd had a blowout on one of the trailer tires and had called Jim's Tire Service in Perryton, who were sending out a man to fix it. Someone needed to meet him at Highway 281 and lead him to the ranch.

Kris and Nikki had driven to the ranch that morning and were at the house site, sifting through the rubble for something that might have survived. Kris had dreaded that task but knew that, the next day, Scot's crew was going to load everything into dump trucks, haul it off, and scrape it down to native soil.

I still had chores to do and thought that Kris and Nikki might not mind taking a break and meeting the serviceman at the highway. I drove the Ranger a mile north to the house site and found them standing in the rubble of what used to be the kitchen.

Kris had tears in her eyes. "John, I know you don't want to hear this, but I'm not ready for Scot to sweep all this away." Forty-nine years of living with her had given me enough sense not to argue. I said, "That's okay, I'll meet the serviceman."

I drove eleven miles to Highway 281 and met the serviceman (it wasn't Felix this time, but another man whose name I don't remember). Back at the barn, he went to work on the flat tire and I went to the cab of Scot's truck.

I needed to have a talk with Tina, and she needed to have a woman-to-woman talk with Kris. Tina had some distance on the loss we had suffered and was able to see the broader view. We had the equivalent of a dead body (three burned structures and three piles of rubble). Scot was viewing it from a practical, masculine perspective: "We need to bury the corpse and we have a big crew coming tomorrow to do it." Kris was expressing the emotions of a grieving woman: "I can't give it up!" I hoped that Tina could bridge the gap and help Kris accept that we had to bury the corpse of her home.

I opened the truck door and was surprised to see my wife sitting in the driver's seat of her son's big Mack truck. Tina and Nikki sat behind her in the sleeper section. The motor was running and the cab was nice and warm. All three of them were eating sandwiches and Kris was smiling.

I felt a big sense of relief. The eyes of Nikki and Tina said, "She's going to be all right."

I climbed into the cab and took the passenger-side seat. Nikki made me a sandwich out of a box-full of meat, cheese, bread, and fixings, and we had a pleasant conversation until Scot banged on the door and, with his usual charm, yelled, "Get out! I've got to go back to Amarillo for another load."

That cleared the cab, and Scot and Tina roared off to get another load of equipment.

We made it back to the town house around seven, and three ladies from the church arrived shortly thereafter with our supper.

SATURDAY, MARCH 11: CLEANUP DAY

When I left the house at 6 that morning, I knew we were in for a cold day. The wind had gone to the north and was blowing strong enough to make it unpleasant. I was glad for the warm clothes I had scrounged from Wilkens.

I drove in the dark to the Maverick Books warehouse on the northwest loop road, where I continued recording the events of my life in the post-fire world. Already the small details—so important to a piece of writing—were beginning to fade and blur.

Around nine o'clock, I got a text from Scot: "Leaving Amarillo." I slipped my Mac and modem into my black shoulder bag and headed south to the ranch, a 45-minute drive.

My pickup had become a temporary home, office, tool shed, and trash receptacle. It contained a sack of dogfood, empty feed sacks, tools, chewing tobacco, paper plates, plastic forks, bills, gloves, extra clothes, boots, bottles of water, a catch rope, and the shoulder bag that contained my Mac, the latest issue of *Livestock Weekly*, a hairbrush and toothbrush, a checkbook, recent mail, and a bottle of Aleve.

To that flotsam I now added a box of Hank paperback books. The newest title, #69, had just arrived at our warehouse and I thought it would be a nice gesture to give Scot and Tina's friends the first copies of the book, autographed by the guy they were coming to help.

When I turned south off of Highway 281, the early slanting sun revealed the desolation the fire had left of the flat country above the caprock. Nothing remained of the tall grass but ash and dust, swept up into an ugly haze by the sharp north wind. That desert of ash stretched nine miles south to the Canadian River and forty miles east to the Oklahoma state line.

On March 7, when Scot had first heard about the fire, he called me at once. "Dad, I'll get it cleaned up. I'll take care of it." Sure enough, he had assembled a small army of workers to clear the rubble of the main house, my office, and the bunkhouse, and he had every intention of finishing the job in two days. He and his friends had brought two big dump trucks, a backhoe, two skid-steer loaders, a mini-excavator, and a D6 Cat dozer.

When I reached the house site, I saw Scot's people sifting through the rubble, among them three women wearing dust masks and several men I hadn't met. I introduced myself and thanked them for leaving their warm homes on a cold, windy Saturday morning and coming to this sad place to help. I was amazed at how cheerful they were.

Months later, I asked Tina to provide me with a list of these Good Samaritans: Kelly and Davy Hamilton; Kami and Jeff Hamilton; Jennifer and Daniel Gleaves; Savanna Keller; Casey Podzimny; J. B. Hamm; Dan Wolfcale; Charlie Stork; Kevin Kelley; Kale Erickson; Doug Wilkens; David Decker; Phil Haynes; Jed Symons; and Ashley, Randy, and ReAnna Wilson.

Scot had mentioned that the Hamiltons had some experience in recovering valuables after a fire. They concentrated their search on the area where Kris had kept her jewelry box and recovered some rings. Later, they found two gold Krugerrands I had kept in a drawer in the bathroom. They also recovered a stash of silver dimes that I had forgotten about.

Those dimes went back to the 1970s. My dad gave each of his three children $10,000 to invest, and I chose to dabble in the silver market. Silver had become an active commodity because Nelson Bunker Hunt, the billionaire from Dallas, was buying huge quantities of it and trying to corner the market. For six months, I bought and sold silver coins through a dealer in the Midwest and made some pretty good money at it.

Those silver dimes the workers found in the rubble were the ones in my possession when Bunker Hunt ran out of cash and credit and the silver market went into a swoon. In the Eighties, Kris and I moved several times, and the sacks of silver went with us. When we built the house on the ranch in 1993, we stashed them at the back of a deep drawer in the kitchen, and I had forgotten about them.

The coins were tarnished from the fire, but they still had value as meltdown silver. Several weeks later, George Chapman sold them to a dealer in Amarillo and we put the proceeds into the new house fund.

MY BURNED OFFICE

Meanwhile, Scot began the cleanup of my writing office, a 10′ x 30′ structure a hundred yards west of the house. I had visited the ruin only once, seeing a surprisingly small lump of debris covered with warped, blackened sheets of roofing metal.

I didn't pick through the rubble of this place where I had done my writing every day for fifteen years. Maybe I should have. Something might have survived: some charred relic made of metal, a few pages of a manuscript I'd written in the Eighties, or a half-burned journal that I'd kept while I was working as a cowboy in the Seventies.

Something might have come through the conflagration, but I lacked either the will or the curiosity to examine the corpse.

It is difficult for someone who reveres the written word to comprehend or express the loss of books, manuscripts, journals, and letters—the accumulation of a lifetime. It's a bit like a brain injury that erases segments of knowledge and memory.

Among the items irretrievably lost were:

> My grandfather's collection of books about Texas and the Southwest.
>
> Books autographed by Elmer Kelton, John Graves, Marc Simmons, Nancy Pearcey, Carl Lane Johnson, Gene Edward Veith, Baxter Black, Ed Ashurst, S. J. Dahlstrom, and others.

Letters from John Graves, Elmer Kelton, J. Evetts Haley, Marc Simmons, Paul F. Boller Jr., Herman Wouk, and a couple of letters I exchanged with Larry McMurtry in 1969.

Two writing awards from the Ranching Heritage Center.

A three-foot-wide shelf of handwritten journal books, every journal I had kept since 1968.

My books on Panhandle archeology, theology, biblical studies, ancient civilizations, and modern physics, which I had underlined, indexed, and annotated in the margins.

Boxes of fan letters I had received over the years.

Two unpublished novels in typescript.

A studio-quality Stelling Staghorn banjo, one of two I lost in the fire, each with a replacement cost of $7,000.

Fifteen years' worth of business receipts and tax records.

A human skull I had bought for $1.50 in an open-air market in Mexico City in 1966. It had reminded me that "All men are like grass, and all their glory is like the flowers of the field."

Four Bibles, three computers, two turtle doves . . .

My office was dead. On Cleanup Day, Scot scooped it up with his tractor, and J. B. Ham hauled it away.

J. EVETTS HALEY

One item that escaped the fire was Grandfather Curry's first-edition copy of J. Evetts Haley's biography of Charles Goodnight, signed by Haley the year it was published. I gave the book to Mark for Christmas in 2015 and I'm glad I did. It was the most valuable book in my library.

I met Mr. Haley one day in 1973, when I had worked up the courage to knock on the door of his home in Canyon, Texas. It required courage because Mr. Haley had a reputation for being a blowtorch of strong political opinions. At that time, I was only a few years out of the University of Texas and Harvard Divinity School and still wore longish curly hair and my best effort at a beard. I had a feeling Mr. Haley wouldn't approve of my appearance and might mistake me for a hippie or a Bolshevik.

I was right; he disliked me on sight. But before he could throw me out of his house, his wife invited me to sit down and stay a while. That gave me the opportunity to reveal my West Texas credentials to the scowling historian.

On the Curry-Sherman side of the family, I had a solid ranching pedigree. In fact, Haley had recounted the murder by Comanches of my great-great-grandmother, Martha Sherman, in his biography of Goodnight (Haley 1949, 49). Also, my rancher/cowboy kin in Gaines County had known the notorious outlaw Tom Ross, and my mother used to walk to school with Ross's daughter in Seminole.

Haley was very familiar with the lore of Tom Ross and had his own thick file of notes about him. My mentioning Ross spilled some water on Haley's embers, but still he growled, "John, you seem a nice kid, but why do you wear those damned whiskers?"

I had come prepared for a cross-examination and explained that I admired Haley's book on Goodnight so much, I grew a beard in imitation of Goodnight's well-known thatch of facial hair. At that point, Mr. Haley ran out of bullets and even smiled. We became friends and exchanged letters over the years.

The fire had also obliterated my personal winery, the place where, for fifteen years, I had made Merlot in six-gallon batches. I bought the grape juice, equipment, and ingredients from a place in Ohio and called the product "M-Cross Merlot."

I'm not a wine connoisseur, but I thought my Merlot was as good as any I had tasted. Anything better would have been wasted on me. Mark and Nathan Dahlstrom seldom missed a chance to make snooty comments about my cowboy wine, but they had consumed plenty of it over the years.

FEEDING CATTLE AND LUNCH IN THE BARN

I had cattle to feed. Tina was sitting in her Jeep in front of the main house and asked if I needed help feeding. Sure, why not? She hopped into the pickup and we loaded fifty-pound sacks of feed at the barn.

My first objective for the morning was to pull the cattle down from the upper west pasture and try to relocate them in the west. The upper west had no grass left, only ash and cinders, and we still didn't have electric power to the submersible pump.

We drove up the long, steep hill that led to the upper west and found no cattle in the spot where we had been feeding them hay. We drove north and east and gave the pasture a thorough search. We saw no cattle. That was good news. They must have figured out that the upper west had nothing to offer them and that the west was a better place to be, now that the fires had burned themselves out.

We drove to the west pasture and found the cattle at the windmill. Tina sat on the flatbed and poured out the feed while I drove, and we continued feeding the other pastures.

By 12, Scot's crew had hauled off the remains of my former office and the bunkhouse, dumping them into a deep draw in the mesa pasture. The pads were level and clean. You might not have guessed that anything had been there. Scot had also dispatched several workers to the barn, with orders to clean it up and toss out anything that didn't have an obvious purpose.

As an adult, Scot had developed a fanaticism about clean barns. His big steel barn and shop outside of Amarillo was almost as clean as the surgical suites in St. Anthony's Hospital: no dirt, no mice, no feed cubes scattered by invading raccoons, no tools out of place, no oil spills. And woe be it to anyone who disturbed the order.

This side of Scot's nature had never showed itself when he was growing up. If we had ever seen him pick up a dirty sock or make his bed, we would have filmed it and sent it to all the kinfolk for their amusement. The magnitude of change in Scot compared to that of Saul on the road to Damascus. Those of us who knew him as a teenager were astounded.

His crew of barn cleaners accomplished in one hour what I had thought about doing for years. They were merciless and hauled off a load of stuff I had accumulated over twenty years. By 1, the barn floor was swept clean, a table had been set up, and we were eating a hot meal catered by Calico County Restaurant: pot roast, mashed potatoes and gravy, broccoli and rice casserole, and green beans, a wild contrast to the cold, dusty, ashy world outside.

THE MAIN HOUSE

After lunch, I gave out copies of the #69 Hank book, then the whole crew moved to the main house and began what I perceived as the monumental task of clearing the ruins of our home: ashes on top of ashes, rock from the fireplace, gas pipes, the charred hulls of the kitchen stove, a big refrigerator, dishwasher, deep freeze, washer and dryer, two hot water heaters, and the entire cement slab laced together with rebar.

Kris and Nikki had arrived at the house site around 10. Our daughter Ashley, her husband Randy, and their daughter ReAnna had come from Canadian, and our grandson Kale Erickson had driven over from Amarillo. While Tina and I were off feeding cattle, they walked through the ruins and shared their memories of good times in the house: Thanksgiving with all the family, Christmas morning, the homeschooling years, making wild plum jelly and salsa in Kris's kitchen, sewing, quilting, singing, and playing chess. They hugged and cried.

Most people would have been intimidated by the task of clearing such a huge pile of rubble and wrecked memories. However, I had been with Scot and Tina when he first went striding through the ruins. He smiled a crazy smile, rubbed his hands together, and said, "I can't wait!"

What an odd response to a catastrophe! Tina and I exchanged glances. She smiled and shrugged. That was Scot, her husband, our son.

For the rest of Saturday afternoon, I stepped back and watched a ballet of men and machines: two dump trucks, two skid-steer loaders, and one backhoe. The drivers had no electronic means of communicating with each other, yet somehow they stayed out of each other's way and never collided. Now and then, I saw them using hand signals, but mostly they seemed to be operating on intuition and experience. They reminded me of bees rebuilding a hive, precise and relentless.

Now and then, the door on Scot's tractor flew open and he leaped out onto the rubber tread, cut loose with a piercing whistle and waved an arm, then dived back into the cab.

Those who were supposed to know what it meant knew what it meant: bring up a dump truck, stop talking, pay attention, get out of the way.

In his youth, Scot was one of those boys who didn't fit the model of American public education. He and the school system went to war on his first day of kindergarten, and it got worse every year. We were told that he had learning disabilities. What we observed was that if he wasn't interested in a subject, you couldn't force him to learn it, but if he wanted to learn something, you couldn't buy enough chains and padlocks to keep him out of it.

In the nineteenth century, boys like Scot attended four or five grades of classroom schooling, at which point someone recognized that you can't make a poodle out of a coyote pup. Those boys became apprentices and learned a trade, went to sea, or set out for the West to find adventure. No doubt some of them robbed banks and stagecoaches, but others became explorers, inventors, soldiers, trail drivers, steamboat captains, ranchers, and entrepreneurs, and nobody noticed or cared that they were slow readers and couldn't spell.

My mother's father and grandfather followed that pattern, each with only a few years of formal education, but they became successful ranchers and solid citizens in West Texas. When they were ready to acquire the skills of language, they taught themselves to read, write, and spell.

In old age, my great-grandfather subscribed to the St. Louis *Post-Dispatch* and kept a book of Shakespeare's plays beside his bed. He had learned to read around a campfire on the Loving ranch in Jack County. My grandfather, Buck Curry, never finished high school but put together an impressive collection of books that occupied three walls of his library, floor to ceiling.

Scot had found a place for a man with his temperament. He acquired practical skills that allowed him to express his unique vision, and here he was at the ruins of our home, directing an army of men and machines like General Patton, accomplishing a task that, to me, would have been impossible.

It is worth noting that General Patton had learning disabilities. He didn't fit into civilian life and probably didn't perform well in school, but he scared the pants off the Nazis. I suspect that when the world begins to unravel and fall apart, we need those boys who have a different way of learning and thinking, the ones we diagnose with ADHD and dyslexia. Maybe God made them that way for a reason.

The next day, Sunday, brought more biting north wind. I did my morning writing and made it out to the ranch around ten. Scot's crew was back at work at the main house, pushing up piles of debris and loading trucks. They had done the "easy" work on Saturday. Now they faced the more difficult task of breaking up the cement slab, cutting or sawing their way through steel rebar, and separating it into chunks they could load into a dump truck with skid-steer loaders.

Around three o'clock, the pad was clean and smooth, the house nothing but a memory in the wind. The workers said their farewells, loaded their machines onto flatbed trailers, and drove back to Amarillo, like a circus that had folded its tents and departed. We never got a bill for the job.

The next day, I sent Scot a note: "Thank you for being a hero at a time when we really needed one."

MARCH 17-20

For several days, I tried to keep to the routine: up before daylight, write at the Maverick Books warehouse until 9, drive to the ranch, and feed hay and cake to all the animals. It wasn't hard work but it made me tired. That was something I had noticed about my post-fire existence: a deep and lingering weariness.

One morning I got a call from a man who was sitting in Canadian with a load of hay. I wasn't sure I needed more hay but wasn't inclined to turn it down, so I gave him directions. When he arrived at the ranch, he introduced me to his shy, smiling twelve-year-old son.

"He's a big Hank fan. When he heard about your loss in the fire, he wanted to bring you some hay. I called around and got your phone number."

They had driven all the way from southern Louisiana, a fourteen-hour journey.

That afternoon, I finished the feeding chores around four and decided to drive up Pickett Canyon, north of the house site, to see what the fire had left around Moonshine Springs and Scott Springs. Before the fire, and for as long as we had owned the ranch, the springs had supported a forest of big cedar trees that reached a height of 30 to 40 feet. Some of them were the size of utility poles.

These were eastern red cedars, not the scrubby one-seed junipers we had on other parts of the ranch. When you cut into one of them with a chain saw, it released a spray of pink chips and the pleasant smell of a cedar chest. Their tops formed a canopy so dense that nothing grew on the ground around them. I would bet that some of those big cedars were a hundred years old, maybe older, and the fact that they had survived so long told me that Pickett Canyon had not seen a major fire in a long time.

What I saw at Moonshine Springs was stark, sad, and almost surreal: charred ashy ground below blackened limbs and trunks. Nothing remained on the limbs. The evergreen canopy had been destroyed by what fire experts call a "crown fire." Those magnificent trees were rare in the Panhandle and none of them survived.

Cedar trees contain an oily sap like turpentine, and they almost explode when they burn. The fire that swept through our canyon must have been extremely hot, and by the time it reached our house, everything in its path was doomed. If we had been caught in our beds or if we had tried to fight it with spades and garden hoses, we would have suffered the same fate as the cedars.

As I was leaving Moonshine Springs, I saw smoke rising from the stump of a big cedar. Eleven days after the fire, it was still smoldering.

On Saturday, I followed my feeding routine but didn't find the west pasture cattle in their usual spot around the windmill. I noticed that they hadn't cleaned up the hay I had put out the day before. I checked the country north of the windmill and didn't see them, so I drove down to the south end and found them across the fence in the pasture that belonged to my neighbors, the Killebrew brothers.

The fence between us had become a mess of burned cedar posts and barbed wire on the ground. I honked the horn, and the cows came over to my side. I poured out two sacks of cake on the ground and unloaded the round bale of grass hay on the flatbed of my pickup.

I was making a sharecropper patch on the fence when two men drove up in a Kawasaki Mule: Wilbur and J. A. Killebrew. They were out checking their fences.

In the twenty-seven years we had owned our ranch, I had never met them. That would seem strange in most places, but not in the Canadian River Valley. Here, ranches are big, rough, and remote, and very few people lived on our side of the river. Wilbur and J. A. had grown up on the ranch but had moved away and now leased their grass to the Haley brothers of Canadian, grandsons of historian J. Evetts Haley.

I had always heard that the Killebrews were tall people, and that proved to be correct. Both brothers must have been 6'5", and J. A. said that the other brother, Flavius, was even taller.

We talked for more than an hour. J. A. said that he wouldn't mind if our cattle stayed on his portion of the ranch, the west side. Some of Wilbur's country to the east had burned, but most of J. A.'s had not. It had a cover of tall grass, sagebrush, and weeds. I was grateful for the offer and said we would probably take him up on it, as Mark and I had worried about our cattle living every day in soot, ash, and dust.

I got back to Perryton around dark, was tired, ate another nice meal from the church ladies, and went to bed early. I slept ten hours, an unusually long time for me.

The next day was Sunday. Kris and Nikki went to church, and I went to the ranch to continue the treadmill routine of feeding cattle cake and hay. Mark was back in Amarillo, where his band, Comanche Moon, had played a fire benefit concert the night before. I ate a sandwich for lunch at the camper, crawled into the bed, and slept for an hour, then lay there for an hour after that. I felt weary.

Wilbur Killebrew called to say that the Haleys wouldn't be turning cattle onto the place until May 15, so we could use it until then. That would take some of the pressure off our country. If the cattle could find roughage in the Killebrew pasture, we wouldn't have to feed them hay every day.

I also got a call from a man named Joe Holley. I recognized the name and knew he was a writer. He said he was now writing a Texas column for the *Houston Chronicle* and was in the Panhandle doing a story on the fires. He wondered if we could get together on Monday. He was going to Lipscomb to interview a good friend of our family, Lance Bussard, and when he got done, he would head for the M-Cross.

When I got back to town, I was glad to see that Kris seemed to be in a cheerful mood and had been talking to Tina about ideas for rebuilding. That was a good sign.

Monday brought another day of feeding stock at the ranch. The weather had changed from cold and windy to hot and windy. Our poor country was so dry, the air was filled with caliche dust from the roads and ash from the fires. At lunchtime, I glanced at myself in the mirror in the trailer. The face reminded me of a character from *Band of Brothers*, a tired man with red eyes and soot on his nose.

Joe Holley caught up with me around two in the afternoon, and we talked while feeding the east pasture in the Ranger. He mentioned that he had grown up in Waco and attended Abilene Christian University and reminded me that he had served as editor of *Texas Co-op Power News*, a magazine published for members of Texas rural electric cooperatives. I had received and read the *Power News* for years, as a member of North Plains Electric Cooperative, and knew it was a good periodical. Indeed, it had the largest circulation of any magazine in Texas.

Joe said that he was going to write a story about the Perryton fire and wanted to do another story on me and my experience. We exchanged business cards and promised to stay in touch, then he drove on to Amarillo. His article, which appeared in the *Chronicle* on April 1, was a good piece of writing and research.

TUESDAY, MARCH 21

We'd had several unusually warm days, and sprigs of green were beginning to show in low spots, ravines, and especially in Pickett Canyon. In none of the pastures had the cattle cleaned up the grass hay I had put out the day before. They might have accepted alfalfa or rye hay, but they were turning up their noses at the grass hay, an indication that they were starting to chase the green grass and weeds. They still needed protein, so I fed cake as usual but didn't put out any round bales until they cleaned up what they had.

I drove back to Perryton to an empty house. Kris and Nikki had gone to Amarillo to buy Kris some clothes, then had supper and spent the night with Scot and Tina. Like me, Kris had been wearing used clothes donated by friends.

I looked through the day's mail, paid some bills, and ate a cold supper out of the refrigerator. I watched an episode of *Sherlock Holmes*, the BBC series starring Jeremy Brett. Our large collection of DVD movies had been destroyed in the fire, but Nikki had ordered new copies of some of our favorites.

I turned off the program at 8:30. It was too early to go to bed, but I felt tired. I sat alone in the silent house and began to experience what I interpreted to be delayed grief. I come from a line of sturdy Protestants who took what life threw at them and moved on. They didn't spend much time grieving and were good at comforting the people who were trying to comfort them.

My father served as a medical staff sergeant on Saipan during World War II. He never talked to me about the war. He never cried, whimpered, told stories, or sought comfort. I didn't have the faintest idea what he did in 1944–1945 in the South Pacific, except that he was the administrator of a field hospital.

Mike Harter, my cousin, did some research on the war in the Pacific, where both our fathers served. He learned that Saipan received the wounded soldiers from the invasion of Iwo Jima—including my friend John Graves, the Texas author. The field hospitals were overwhelmed with wounded. Everyone on the staff was giving injections, hooking up IVs, carrying bedpans, mopping up blood, and covering corpses.

It must have been a horrible experience, but Joe Erickson never said a word about it to me.

After the fire, I became adept at telling friends, "We're going to be all right." I had been saying that for two weeks. Now, in the silent house in town, I wondered if it were true. I felt remote, scattered, rootless, like an ant whose mound had been destroyed by a road grader. All the rhythms of my life, pre-fire, had been disrupted, and those rhythms had been crucial to my sense of worth, accomplishment, and equilibrium—in ways I was just beginning to comprehend.

WEDNESDAY, MARCH 22

In the morning, I met Mark at the ranch, where we talked about the immediate future: our supply of hay and feed, rebuilding fences, and moving cattle to unburned pastures. Our friend George Chapman had offered pasture around Amarillo, so we decided to ship the yearlings to him on Friday.

Today, our objectives were to sort off fourteen yearlings from the west pasture bunch and haul them back to the mesa pasture where they belonged. We called the cattle into a small set of wire pens that had been partially destroyed in the fire, sorted off the cows and calves, and loaded the fourteen yearlings into the 24-foot gooseneck trailer.

The day of the fire, our two stock trailers had been parked in a short-grass flat southwest of the house, and the fire had burned the grass around them. We weren't sure if the tires had been damaged. They didn't appear to be burned, but there was a chance that we would get a nasty surprise when we started back to the main pens with a load of yearlings—the tires might fly apart. But we got lucky.

That done, Mark wanted to move the west cows to the unburned Killebrew pasture to the south. The brothers had given us permission to park some cattle on their place until May 15, and that arrangement would give us two months to plan a long-term solution.

While I fed the bulls up in the canyon, Mark saddled Glendore, his Arabian gelding, and pulled on a pair of secondhand shotgun chaps he had bought at Oliver's Saddle Shop in Amarillo to replace the ones he had lost in the fire. I was surprised that he had found chaps to fit him. He was a big man, 6'5", and had muscular thighs.

He had also picked up a new set of spur straps to replace ones that burned in the fire. He attached the Oliver straps to the charred spurs he had found in the ruins of the house.

I loaded sacks of feed into the back of the Ranger and drove to the west pasture with Mark's blue heeler, Lena. Mark followed, riding Glendore. We found the cows at the windmill. I called the cows and set a course straight south, to the gate into the Killebrew country. The cattle followed, twenty-three cows and fifteen calves. Mark came along behind, making sure that we didn't leave any small calves.

That is always a danger when you call cattle from a vehicle. Sometimes small calves will be lying down behind a sagebrush or will get tired on a drive and separate from their mothers. Cows are smart enough to sort things out if you leave the gates open, but we hoped to avoid any separations.

Most of the cows followed me through the gate or picked their way across a space in the fence that had been destroyed by the fire. As could be expected, two calves missed the gate and Mark had to herd them to a point where they built their own gate—that is, went through the fence—and got back with their mamas.

There was no road on this end of the Killebrew place, but during the fire a bulldozer had cut a path for the fire trucks, so I followed the dozer track through sand hills and sagebrush, toward a windmill two miles away. It was the only water source we were sure about. I had checked it several days before and knew it had a full tank of water.

When you move cattle to a new pasture, you take them to water, feed them, and give them time to settle down and pair up. You want them to know where the water is.

When we left the Killebrew windmill, the cows had started grazing not far from the water tank. For the first time in two weeks, they had pasture that wasn't black and didn't smell of smoke.

Mark rode back to the corrals, about five miles away, and checked out the lay of the land. We didn't know this Killebrew country and needed to get familiar with it. I drove back to the barn, loaded three sacks of feed, and went east to feed that pasture. Later, we met at the camper.

I had decided to spend the night at the ranch, sharing the camper with Mark. He had brought his propane barbecue grill and some venison steaks and sausage, and he cooked them outside the camper. He also brought the makings for a green salad. For a bachelor, he was a pretty good chef.

I got the bed, and Mark slept on a cot. I slept well.

THURSDAY, MARCH 23

We didn't wake up until 7:30, after daylight. Mark had his morning agenda of things to do and calls to make. He stayed in the trailer while I drove a mile north up the canyon. I wanted to spend some time at the place where I had done my writing for many years and to experience the smells and sounds of morning in Pickett Canyon.

The air was more humid than usual and thin clouds washed over the sky. The weather report on the radio predicted a chance of rain. The heavy air held the very familiar smell of burned grass, which greeted me the moment I stepped out of the pickup.

The buffalo grass in front of my former office had burned but was showing a tint of green, and sprigs of cheat grass had popped up in the dry ravine that, on maps, is called Pickett Ranch Creek.

On the steep canyon walls, I could see the skeletons of charred junipers and the yellowed remains of cactus. That was one positive result of the fire. We had way too much cactus on the place, and I had spent years spraying it from a four-wheeler. In two or three hours, the fire had accomplished a job that would have occupied me for a hundred years on a four-wheeler spray rig.

The day after the fire, I had noticed a total absence of birds, but they had moved back into the canyon and were singing and chirping in the burned limbs of cedar trees. I recognized the coo of mourning doves (how appropriate for the scene, "mourning"), the whistle of cardinals, the rattle of two wood-peckers, and the songs of other birds I couldn't identify.

After my writing time, Mark and I discussed the day's work. He was still trying to finish up a contract for a client in Amarillo, so we decided that I should take the Ranger over to the Killebrew pasture to make sure the cows had stayed close to water. I found them near the windmill, poured out two sacks of feed, and headed back.

In the west pasture, I drove up on nine yearlings at the windmill. They were supposed to be in the mesa pasture but had walked across a burned fence into the west. Since we hoped to ship all the yearlings to pasture near Amarillo the next day, this was irritating in the extreme. Furthermore, they were finding just enough cheat grass not to be very interested in following a feed wagon, and it took me an hour to coax them up the hill at Indian Springs and down into the mesa pasture.

MORE FIRE

By that time, the wind had kicked up to 35–40 miles an hour, with higher gusts, and the air was filled with a mixture of caliche dust off the roads and soot from the burned pastures.

Mark was at the corrals. As I pulled up, I smelled smoke and so did he. Good grief, did we have another fire in the valley?

We jumped into the Ranger and roared to a high spot on the south end of the mesa pasture. There, we could see smoke rising on the horizon, due south of us on the other side of the river. The wind seemed to be out of the southeast, and it was blowing hard. In that wind, any fire had to be taken seriously, and the fact that we smelled smoke was a bad sign. When you smell the smoke, you might be in danger.

The day before, we had moved our cows onto the Killebrew, an expanse of tall, dry grass, and Mark wanted to take a horse over there and move them back to our west pasture, which was already burned.

I called Starla Nicholson, our neighbor on the C Bar C ranch, and asked what she knew about the fire. She said it had started west of Miami and was out of control. She suggested that we had better evacuate. I agreed, remembering that in one of the fires two weeks before, three young people had died trying to move cattle. I wasn't ready to lose Mark.

We sped back to the corral. While Mark went to the trailer and packed his belongings and loaded them in his pickup, I opened all the gates in the corrals and turned five horses and three heifers up into Pickett Canyon. That canyon had already burned, and we had spring water on the north end. Maybe they would be safe, if there was such a thing as a safe place.

We loaded the dogs, Lena and Daisy, and left the ranch in our two pickups. At the top of the caprock on Tandy Road, we parked and watched the clouds of smoke on the southern horizon. They were getting bigger. Mark called some of the neighboring ranchers, in case they weren't aware of the fire.

The blaze appeared to be moving to the northwest, which would keep it off what remained of our grass, and off the Killebrew pasture, but one of the characteristics of March weather is that the wind changes directions. That is usually the way firefighters get burned: they're spraying water on a fire that suddenly turns around and comes after them.

That's why you should run from a fire in a 40-mph wind, regardless of where you think it might be going.

We watched the fire until six o'clock. Mark stayed a while longer, and I drove back to town. I'd had enough for one day. My bath water that evening was the usual brown with streaks of black.

Mark joined us at the town house around 7. We had brought the dogs, Lena and Daisy, and they were filthy. Kris and Nikki gave them a bath, then walked them on the street until they dried off. By this time, the air in town was heavy with the smell of grass smoke.

After supper, Mark made some calls to check on the fire, which had been given the name Rankin Road fire. It had jumped the Canadian River and was on the C Bar C ranch, heading to the northwest. It had crossed from Roberts County into Ochiltree County and burned some of the Wilson ranch, which joined us on the west side. Law enforcement had closed Highway 70 between Perryton and Pampa, and also Highway 281, the road Mark and I had just taken into town.

When Mark talked to Starla Nicholson around 9, Dave was still out with the fire truck, and she had evacuated her house and driven to Pampa. Now the highway was closed and she couldn't get back home.

Once again, we had a troubled sleep, worrying about the cows we had moved to the Killebrew pasture and wondering if they would be alive, maimed, or dead come morning. Would this ever end?

FRIDAY, MARCH 24

I slept until 7 and drove to the Maverick Books warehouse to put in a few hours of writing. The weather had turned cool again, so I wore the vest Doug Wilkens had given me and a jacket donated by George Chapman.

Mark had stayed in a motel (our house in town was pretty small) and called me at 9, saying he was heading to the ranch. He had heard that Roberts County had gotten enough rain in the night to put out the fire. A cold front had blown in after dark, and the wind had shifted around to the north.

If the cold front hadn't brought rain, the fire would have reversed direction and burned another path to the south or southeast, possibly burning for days. The firefighters got a good break with the rain.

I drove to the town house to say hello to Kris and goodbye to Nikki. She had to drive back to San Antonio. I thanked her for being such a help and comfort to Kris. I don't know what we would have done without her.

I filled up the pickup with diesel and bought a bag of ice, just in case the previous day's fires had knocked out electricity at the ranch again. Mark had stocked the camper's refrigerator with groceries, and we didn't want to lose them due to loss of refrigeration. Between the ice storm in January and the fires of 2017, we had learned to think about electricity, which most Americans take for granted. When you turn on a light switch, you get a light. If your deep freeze is stocked with beef, it will remain frozen.

Instead of taking the usual route to the ranch (turning east on Highway 281 at the twenty-one-mile corner), I continued south on 70 toward the Canadian River Bridge. Beyond the twenty-one-mile corner, I saw blackened pastures on the east side of the highway. It appeared that the Rankin Road fire had burned through Sourdough Canyon on the Flowers and Courson ranches but had not damaged Eric Phillips' house on the west side of the highway.

I passed two semi-trucks parked on the side of the road, each with a big John Deere dozer on a flatbed trailer. The dozers belonged to the Texas Forest Service and had been plowing fireguards and trails for the fire trucks.

Driving down the caprock, I saw a gash of black in the C Bar C's Battleship Rock pasture, west of the highway. The fire had jumped the roadway and would have gone a long distance to the northwest if it hadn't been stopped by the rain. The fire had burned all of the C Bar C pasture east of the highway, as far as I could see, and appeared to have burned a lot of Boone Pickens' grass on the other side of the river.

Down in the bottom of the valley, I was relieved to see that Dave and Starla Nicholson's house had survived, but the fire had gotten close. If the wind had shifted just a bit, if the rain hadn't come when it did, they might have been wiped out.

I turned east on North River Road and drove through the burned C Bar C country. I saw two spots of smoking debris in the ditch and passed four Forest Service vehicles with "FIRE" written on the doors.

As I drove east, my main concern was the Killebrew country, where we had driven our cows and calves. The Rankin Road fire had burned the south end of the Killebrew ranch on both sides of the county road. The big question was, how far north did it go?

It didn't look good, and I had to start thinking about what Mark and I would do if we found cattle that had been burned.

I had no experience with that kind of disaster but had been hearing a lot about it: cows with burned feet or blistered milk bags; cows that had lost their calves and calves that had lost their mothers; cows that had been blinded.

Ranchers east of us in Lipscomb and Hemphill Counties were living with that nightmare. In their flat, tall-grass country, the fire of March 6 had moved so fast that cattle couldn't escape, and now ranchers were having to doctor the ones that could be saved and shooting the ones that were beyond help.

It suddenly occurred to me that the March 6 fire had destroyed all my pistols, rifles, shotguns, and ammunition. I didn't own a firearm anymore, so if we had to shoot damaged cattle, I would have to borrow a rifle.

Those thoughts were hanging over me when I got a call from Mark. The cell phone service was always chancy in that part of the valley, but I heard enough to brighten my mood. He had driven north on the Killebrew ranch, far enough to see that our cows were safe. That was wonderful news.

We joined up at the camp trailer and discussed the day's work. The previous day, before the fire had sent us scrambling, we had planned to ship all our yearlings to George Chapman's country north of Amarillo. Mark had called the trucker and had everything lined up to ship today, around noon. That plan had been put on hold by the Rankin Road fire, but now it appeared we might be able to do it.

Mark saddled Glendore. I loaded two sacks of cake onto the flatbed pickup and drove south to locate the yearlings. I found them on some unburned grass, about a mile from the pens. I honked the horn and started them north. Mark rode behind them to push the slow ones, and we pulled and pushed them into the pens. I fed them some cake. They had water and a round bale of good rye hay.

Mark, the space-age cowboy, had already called the trucker in Amarillo and told him to head our way. He had even given him a "pin" for his navigation program, locating our exact position on the ranch. He had done all of this with his cell phone, on horseback.

While we waited for the truck, Mark gathered a small bunch of bulls and heifers that we had parked in Pickett Canyon. We loaded them into the 24' gooseneck, hauled them around to the east pasture, and gave that bunch three sacks of cake.

We had enough time for lunch, so Mark fired up the propane grill and cooked the last of the venison he had brought. He even produced another salad from the refrigerator, so we had a pretty fancy lunch: broiled venison and salad, eaten on a picnic table in front of the camper trailer on a cold day in March, breathing air still heavy with the smell of fire.

The truck driver arrived around 3 in a big Peterbilt truck with "Dee King Trucking" painted on the side. He backed up to the chute and we loaded forty-five yearlings and sent them to Chapman's pasture north of Amarillo. Mark had to go back to Amarillo, so he led the way and was present to unload the stock.

We never received a bill from Dee King Trucking.

After they left, I made a few phone calls, one of them to Burk Adcock, our neighbor to the south. Burk and his wife Kim lived on a ranch west of Miami, near the spot where yesterday's Rankin Road fire had started. I had heard that the fire missed their house, but I knew that Burk had lost some pasture on his leased country that joined us on the south.

Several days before, he had offered to let us move some of our cattle onto his country. I had a feeling that things had changed with yesterday's fire, and I was right. Burk apologized and explained that he would need the pasture he had offered to us. I understood and told him not to worry about it. We were all scrambling to care for our livestock, and the rules of the game were changing with every shift of the wind.

Speaking of wind, while I was talking to Burk, I noticed that the wind had shifted to the north and was really kicking up the dust. This was a cold front that had been predicted. The weather forecasters expected wind gusts up to sixty miles an hour. By now, that kind of wind sent shivers through every rancher in the Panhandle, but the cold front had some moisture in it, which lessened the fire danger. And I had nothing left to burn anyway.

Later, on the way back to town, I saw that the burned country above the caprock was blowing dust and ash, and it made a sad picture. But it began to rain, and Mark texted that he had encountered rain on the way to Amarillo.

FIRE AND ARCHEOLOGY

Instead of going to the town house, I drove out north of Perryton to Doug Wilkens' place in the country. He had sent me pictures of some prehistoric artifacts he had salvaged from the ruins of our burned house, the day Scot launched his cleanup campaign. They were the remains of my artifact collection from sites on the ranch.

I had spent three decades collecting those artifacts (dart points, arrow points, scrapers, drills, knives, and sherds of pottery), and had kept them in small plastic bags, separated by site and location. The logic behind the system was that an artifact without provenience (the history of where it came from) was just a trinket that yielded no information.

The fire had destroyed my bags and boxes and thus my filing system, but somehow in my post-fire stupor it didn't occur to me that the artifacts themselves would have survived.

Wilkens, with a clearer head, knew where in the house I had kept them and had the presence of mind to sift through the rubble and salvage them.

He was an "amateur" archeologist, meaning that he didn't study archeology in college or take an advanced degree in the subject. But over the past thirty-five years, he had worked beside professional archeologists on a number of excavations in the Panhandle and had built a reputation as a passionate, careful, well-informed archeologist. He was a steward with the Texas Historical Commission and had been involved in controlled excavations on the M-Cross ranch for twenty-five years.

When I entered his office, I saw that he had cleaned the artifacts and organized them by type (arrow points, dart points, ceramics, flint tools), laid out on his table. He asked about a small group of dart points. Did I remember where I had found them?

"Yes, they all came from a cut bank in the east pasture, south of the pond. I found them in the same place, on the same day, and never found any more points at that spot."

He wrote it down on a piece of paper. "That's what I wanted to know."

Now that Wilkens had retired from BP oil company, he spent much of his time following his passion, Panhandle archeology, and especially the archeology of M-Cross ranch. His interest dated back to 1990, the year we bought the place, when Wilkens and an archeologist from Austin, Wayne Bartholomew, conducted a survey of the ranch and recorded sites that showed surface evidence of habitation.

In 1996, Wilkens brought Billy Harrison and Rolla Shaller from the Panhandle–Plains Historical Museum to excavate an unusual site that turned out to be a secondary cremation burial—as far as I know, the only one ever recorded in the Panhandle.

In 2000, Wilkens brought Doug Boyd, a professional archeologist from Austin, to excavate a burned house that dated to AD 1300. A few years later, he brought in Brett Cruse, Charles Frederick, and other respected professionals to excavate five more prehistoric structures.*

Under the influence of Wilkens, I developed a passion for Panhandle archeology and a powerful desire to be a good steward of the prehistoric sites on the ranch. We had a number of them, especially in west pasture. Most of the sites lay buried under 12–18 inches of soil and were almost invisible on the surface.

Over the years, I spent many hours walking over the ranch and looking for subtle evidence of human occupation: stones that were out of context, irregular patterns of vegetation, outcroppings of ash and charcoal, and bits of cultural debris that had been brought to the surface by gophers.

With help from Wilkens, Boyd, Cruse, and Frederick, I acquired a good library of books and articles on archeology of the Southern Plains and kept them in my writing office, three shelves of material that would have stretched out to about nine feet. I read most of those books and articles, and our team carried on lively discussions about Panhandle archeology. Unfortunately, my reference library had been destroyed in the fire.

As I was leaving, Wilkens handed me a copy of an archeological journal he had just received in the mail. It contained two articles, one written by Charles Frederick and the other by Doug Wilkens. They had been working on the articles for at least a year, and here they were at last, in *Transactions of the 51st Regional Archeological Symposium for Southeastern New Mexico and Western Texas.*

---

* https://www.texasbeyondhistory.net/villagers/hank1/index.html

In their papers, Wilkens and Frederick presented evidence that two houses we excavated between 2000 and 2004, and which dated to approximately AD 1300, were dirt-covered pithouses: earth lodges.

In professional circles, this was a controversial hypothesis. Archeologists had been studying Plains Village ruins in the Panhandle for more than a century, but nobody had ever found an earth lodge or had even suspected one might exist. The earth lodge was a common house type in Upper Republican sites in Kansas, Nebraska, and the Dakotas, and most archeologists doubted that they had ever appeared in our area on the Southern Plains.

Well, they did, and our team had assembled the data to prove it. The presence of earth lodges in our region answered a question that had bothered us since the fires of 2006 and especially after the 2017 fire: How did prehistoric people survive such enormous fires? At least part of the answer lay in house design. The earth lodge was immune to fires outside the house.

MARCH 25-APRIL 1

The next day, after my writing time, I drove down to the ranch to feed hay and cake to the east pasture cows and to the bunch we had moved onto the Killebrew pasture. I was anxious to see the cows on the Killebrew, as I hadn't fed or seen them since the Rankin Road fire the previous Thursday.

As I drove through the mesa pasture, on my way to the barn, I was surprised to see red Bonsmara cows. How could that be? The day before, Mark and I had emptied the mesa pasture when we shipped the yearlings to Amarillo.

Then it occurred to me that the cattle on Killebrew had found their way back home, perhaps spooked by the Thursday fires that had come very close to them. I had to smile. Those cows had rubbed out all the work Mark and I had done on Wednesday, but it might turn out for the best. Until we got some rain, every pasture with tall grass had the potential of becoming a death trap, and the Killebrew place had enough fuel to make a big barbecue of our cow herd.

Our place didn't have much grass left to burn, which gave us a kind of King's X during the remainder of the fire season. We had a good supply of hay and cake, and cheat grass was popping out of the charred ground. We would be all right for a while.

I put out hay for both pastures and went to the camper for a lunch break. I dined on the cold leftovers of Mark's venison, which he had been generous enough to leave for me. We agreed it was the best venison we had ever eaten, a young spike buck Mark had bagged in the far west pasture. He had cooked it on the grill with garlic salt and pepper.

I took a nap, then drove up into Pickett Canyon to feed the horses. I was a little surprised to find them still there. They didn't like the canyon and seldom stayed more than a few days before climbing out on a deer trail and going back to their chosen place, the upper west pasture. But this time they had stayed, and it made good sense. The upper west had been burned down to the dirt, and the canyon was always the best source of early grass.

I made it back to Perryton at four o'clock and had some time to go through the mail. We had received a number of cards from people in the local community and large envelopes filled with notes from school children in Texas, Oklahoma, and as far away as Arizona and California. These kids were readers of the Hank books and must have heard about the fires on the news or social media.

I wasn't able to read all the letters, but I did open a few. One came from a ten-year-old boy in Lubbock. He enclosed a ten-dollar gift card from Dairy Queen and advised me that an M&M's Blizzard would help me forget about the fire.

THE DOGCATCHER AND CHURCH

Sunday morning, I was feeling comfortable enough about our situation at the ranch to skip a day of feeding and go to church. In the twenty days since the fire, I had missed Sunday services and Wednesday evening choir practice, having spent most of my time alone with cattle and dogs.

Through it all, our church family had watched after us as a quiet force, providing meals, clothes, and furniture. They had sent cards and text messages, and some had sent money. I had ambivalent feelings about accepting money. When almost everything you once owned is swept away, you respond in different ways.

I am stripped naked, a sparrow in winter.

I am suddenly relieved of the burden of "things," and maybe I didn't need them anyway.

On the other hand, we will have to replace some of those "things" (toenail clippers, deep freezer, vacuum sweeper, cooking pots, furniture, kitchen knives, generator, banjo, warm clothes, boots, hats), as well as a house to hold them, and the cost adds up.

If we rebuild the house, bunkhouse, and my office, it's going to be expensive. Insurance rarely covers replacement costs.

Was I too proud to accept help from people who cared about us? Probably. Yes. I didn't know if we needed cash donations or not. Who can know in the swirl of events that follow a fire? Maybe we would need the help. If we didn't, we could always donate it to the Perryton or Canadian Fire Department.

While I was taking a bath and preparing for church, Kris turned Lena and Daisy outside to take care of their morning necessaries. At the ranch, they stayed outside and we never had to think about it, but we had become town-dwellers, and in Perryton, you're not supposed to let your dogs run loose.

I had just pulled on my clothes when I heard the doorbell ring. Through the glass door, I saw a stern young man in a brown uniform: the dogcatcher. He was holding Lena. Our mutts had been in violation of the Perryton dog laws a mere ten minutes, but somehow they had fallen into the hands of the authorities. It seemed uncommonly bad luck.

He was a young man but had a very serious countenance. I explained that our ranch and home had burned and so forth, hoping to touch his heart. His face showed no emotion. I made an effort to bring some humor to the situation and that fell flat.

He handed me Lena and fetched Daisy from his truck. Daisy, the yellow Lab, was as happy as ever, totally unaware that she had become a felon. She'd been happy running wild in town, happy riding in the dogcatcher's truck, and now was happy to be back to the place where she'd spent a few nights.

Daisy was a big dog, a country dog, not blessed with great intelligence, and prone to willful behavior. Obviously, she would be staying at the ranch from now on.

He didn't write me a ticket, but I got the impression that I shouldn't count on lenience from the authorities a second time. Another violation would bring ominous consequences.

We put the dogs in the garage and went to church. I showed up in the choir room, wearing a shirt donated by Roy Lynn Stollings, jeans from Bill Dudley, a jacket from Doug Wilkens, a nice felt hat from George Chapman, and a pair of shoes Tina had bought at the Red Wing store in Amarillo. I was a miniature United Nations.

It was good to be back in our church community. Later, Kris told me that our friends were glad to see me smiling, not hunched and hollow-eyed. If they had seen me two weeks before, they might have been alarmed. Several times, I had noticed my shadow in profile and had observed the posture of an old man, bent under a load.

Our church observes the liturgy that leads up to the trial, crucifixion, and resurrection of Christ: Palm Sunday, Maundy Thursday, Good Friday, and Easter morning. Those rituals seemed especially relevant after the events of March 2017 and gave some perspective to our hardships of the past two weeks.

If you think wildfires are bad, how would you like to be arrested by stone-faced Roman soldiers (even more sinister than the dogcatcher), betrayed by your best friends, charged with spurious crimes, hailed as "King of the Jews" in a cruel charade of a trial, beaten with a whip that the Romans wouldn't have used on a donkey, and then nailed to a railroad tie, while your mother watched you suffer and die?

The older I get, the more wisdom I extract from that story. It's the same story that, as children, we heard in Sunday school, but it seems to grow in the way our physical bodies evolve from small limbs and small brains, from baby teeth, from tiny voices and corn-silk hair, into adults who bear a scant resemblance to what we used to be. The Easter story has that quality of acquiring depth through time.

After church, Ken and Sandra Splawn invited us to have lunch with them at Chihua's Mexican Restaurant. That seemed appropriate, since we'd been eating supper with them on the evening of March 6 when the fires were sprinting toward our house. Ken insisted that he would be picking up the check, but he didn't get the chance. Someone else in the restaurant paid our bill.

We weren't sure who picked up the tab but suspected Rocky and Janet Tregellas, members of our church. They ranched on Wolf Creek, and the fires had missed them.

NEW WEEK AND RAIN

Monday morning I got up early and went to the warehouse to write, then drove to the ranch with Lena and Daisy. Mark had left Lena with us, knowing that she provided comfort and companionship. She was a sweet dog, polite and observant of people, and she had acquired privileges in our house that no dog before her had ever enjoyed. She had even been *sleeping on our bed!*

I was two cows short on my count in the mesa pasture (the cows that had returned from the Killebrew pasture), so the dogs and I got into the Ranger and drove to the west pasture. I thought the cows might have gotten separated from the main bunch and drifted across the burned fence. I saw no cows or fresh tracks around the windmill, so we drove down to the windmill on the Killebrew place. Same story there: no cows and no fresh tracks.

Maybe they had drifted south on the Killebrew place. If so, they could have gone all the way to the river, and we might not find them for weeks. As long as they found water, they would survive. Or maybe they had died from the delayed effects of the fire.

After a bite of lunch and a nap, I drove the Ranger up the canyon and fed the horses some cake. I noticed that the hackberry trees were starting to bud out, and was surprised, again, how the place was greening up. Even without a good spring rain, the cheat grass was popping out of the ashes, and the permanent grasses (buffalo, grama, and bluestem) were sending out blades of green. The topsoil was as dry as gunpowder, but there must have been some deep moisture left over from the 3" rain we got in January.

On Tuesday, the word on the mind of everyone in the northeastern Panhandle was "rain." The forecast for the next two days called for 100 percent chance and that was welcome news, to put it mildly. Ranchers like me, who had been burned out, needed a good rain to bring back the grass and keep the powder-dry topsoil from blowing. Ranchers who had escaped the fires would not be out of danger until hundreds of thousands of acres of dry fuel got too wet to burn.

The cows in the mesa pasture hadn't cleaned up their round bale of grass hay, so I fed them only cake. I got a good count (twenty-four cows, sixteen calves), which meant we were still short two cows. I drove over to the west pasture to see if they might have showed up at the windmill but didn't find them.

Those two cows finally turned up the next day in the east pasture. I wasn't sure how they got there, but all our fences were in bad shape, so somehow they found their way back to the herd.

FENCING

From there, I drove up the long steep hill to the upper west, went to the north end, and looked at the fence. In the weeks after the fire, the fencing situation had loomed as a major problem, not only for us but for all the ranchers who had been hit by the fire.

Our ranch had fifteen miles of outside fence that we shared with the Adams, Killebrew, Wilson, Cook, Longhoefer, and Brownlee families. Mark had gone out in the Ranger and looked at the fences. A few spots hadn't burned, but most of it had experienced a hot fire and we considered it a total loss. We would have to replace most, if not all, of our perimeter fences.

The most obvious damage you see in a burned fence is the loss of wooden posts. All of the original fencing on our ranch, and in the entire Panhandle, had used cedar posts. Over the years, we had replaced some of the old posts with steel T-posts. The steel posts had survived the fire, but most of the wooden posts had either burned up entirely or suffered enough damage to be useless.

We wondered about the wire. Could burned wire be repaired and stretched? I had heard from several sources that burned wire loses its tensile strength. It becomes brittle. As long as nothing disturbs it, as long as it doesn't break, as long as you don't have to splice and repair the wire, it gives the impression of being a good fence, even though it shows the discoloration of fire.

But here is the problem. Let us suppose that, to save money, two rancher-neighbors decide they don't want to pay a fence builder $11,000–$15,000 per mile to replace the fence. Things rock along just fine for six months until a herd of elk comes along, as they did on my place in 2015.

Deer jump over a barbed wire fence. Antelope scoot under it. These elk plowed right through it, and I found four bent steel posts and barbed wire that had broken in three spots. My son-in-law replaced the posts, spliced the broken wires, and gave each strand a good stretch with fence stretchers. He was able to make repairs because the wire held a splice.

With burned wire, you might not be able to make a loop in the wire to form a splice. The wire is so brittle, it breaks. You cut off the loop and try to build another, but it also breaks. On and on, until you realize that you have nothing to splice. The old wire is useless because you can't repair it. You have to go back to the fence corners and lay out at least one new wire, and you might end up replacing the whole fence.

Mark stepped in and started handling all the calls about fence repair, deciding that we should replace all wooden posts and all wires that had been burned. Two of our neighbors wanted to rebuild the fence with their own employees (we shared the cost of material) and another chose to use a contractor in Perryton.

Mark lined up a fencing contractor from Alanreed, José Álvarez, to rebuild the remaining eight miles of our fence. José had been referred to us by George Chapman, who said he did excellent work.

That estimation turned out to be correct, and I developed tremendous respect for José, a handsome, sturdy man of about fifty. Over a three-month period, he and his men worked in rain, wind, and hundred-degree heat, tore out eight miles of burned fence, and replaced it with new fence that was perfectly straight and tight, using an ancient tractor and old pickups that required constant repairs.

I was never sure where they stayed at night but knew that at least some of the time they slept in their pickups and cooked their meals on campfires. They worked in some of the roughest canyon country in the northern Panhandle, canyons that were not accessible to machinery. José and his men had to climb down on ropes and lower rolls of barbed wire, steel H-brace corners, eighty-pound sacks of cement mix, and water into the canyon bottoms. I don't know how they did it.

José didn't speak a lot of English, so we usually conversed in Spanish (Mark and I carried English–Spanish dictionaries in our vehicles). When José came around to settle up on the job, I tried to tell him, in my best Spanish, how much I admired him for all the things he could do.

In my younger days, I took pride in doing hard physical work and being able to endure heat and cold, but on the best day of my life, I would have been challenged to work beside

José Álvarez for a couple of hours. And never, not in a thousand years, could I have built the kind of fence he produced: as straight and tight as the strings on my banjo.

RAIN

I went back down into the valley, ate a quick lunch of cold venison sausage, and drove up into Pickett Canyon, north of the house. For as long as we'd had the ranch, this canyon pasture had been choked with cactus and yucca. The previous owners of the property had leased it out during the droughts of the Thirties and Fifties, and I assumed that the yucca and cactus were evidence of overgrazing during those bad times.

In a drought, if you have to abuse some of your pastures, you're inclined to overstock the leased land to take the pressure off your own acres.

It appeared that the fire might have done a thorough job of brush control. I was glad to see the burned stubs of yucca and yellowed clusters of cactus, in quantities that surprised me. Standing grass tends to hide the cactus. The fire had swept the landscape clean of grass, and I was looking at tons of dead cactus petals.

The day had begun cloudy and cold, with a sharp north wind. By three o'clock, a misting rain had started, and on the way back to town I drove through rain all the way. It continued through the night and into Wednesday, bringing us the blessing we had needed.

For the first time in a month, ranchers in our area were not scanning the horizon for plumes of white smoke or wondering if they would have to run for their lives.

Slow rain continued through the night and all the next day until six o'clock. I had to exercise discipline to keep from going to the ranch, resisting the rancher impulse to drive through pastures after a rain and take note of every sprig of fresh grass. The roads would be mushy, and there was little I could accomplish.

I spent a restless day in town, catching up on bookkeeping, answering some letters we had gotten from friends, and buying a few items. At seven, we went to choir practice, the first I had attended since the fire. There, I heard reports that Perryton had gotten two inches of rain.

Thursday morning brought clear skies and crisp, damp air. Puddles of water stood in the ditches and low spots around town. For us, the fire season of 2017 had ended, and the time of healing had begun. Too bad the rain hadn't come three weeks sooner.

APRIL 11-12

After doing my morning writing, I drove down to the ranch, loaded sacks of feed in the Ranger, and drove south from the barn. In the five weeks since the fire, and especially since the rains, the ranch had lost most of its dark, sooty coloration and had acquired a greenish tint.

The mesa pasture cattle were grazing in some low sandy hills, south of the county road. They saw me, lifted their heads, and watched, but for the first time since I had begun the winter feeding routine in November, they didn't come running when I appeared.

They were finding enough cheat grass and weeds to satisfy their appetites and weren't interested in the bale of grass hay I had put out several days before. I had to drive into the middle of them before they showed an interest in the sacked feed. When I poured it out on the ground, they were glad to eat it, but their appetite for supplemental feeding had dropped after the rain and several days of sunshine.

In the east pasture, I got an even cooler response. Those cattle had stayed in one bunch throughout the winter months and had always been waiting for me near the wire pens, where I fed them. Today, there were none at the usual feed ground and they had scattered all over the 2,000-acre pasture.

Most of them had moved to the flat country above the caprock, which surprised me. I didn't expect them to leave the lower country, where cheat grass was popping up in the draws, but they were on top and seemed to be finding plenty to eat.

The combination of rain and warm weather was bringing the feeding season to a close. Our plan for the rest of the spring, insofar as we had a plan, was to keep the cows on the ranch for a month or so and let them graze the early grass and weeds, then move at least some of them to country north of Amarillo.

NEW OFFICE, NEW DOG

Scot had been looking around for a small portable building to replace my writing office that had burned. He found one near Amarillo and sent me pictures. It had one main room with cedar paneling and a wood floor, a small kitchen area with a sink and stove, a bathroom, a small loft for sleeping, and a nice little screened porch. The outside was covered with log-veneer siding that gave it a rustic look that fit with our country.

The building belonged to Knut Mjolhus, a friend of Scot's, who offered to sell it. Knut was the owner of Panhandle Steel Erectors and an enthusiastic amateur pilot who owned several planes and a helicopter.

Around two o'clock, I got a call from Scot. He announced that my office was on the way to the ranch. He and Mark would be coming with Knut in his helicopter. I hadn't expected this to happen so soon, but maybe I should have. Scot moved fast.

When Knut's helicopter landed on a grassy area near the old house site, Scot emerged holding a red heeler pup. He and Mark had decided that, in this sad time, Kris and I needed a dog to keep our spirits up and to replace Dixie, the heeler we had lost in the fire. Mark had been kind enough to loan us Lena, but he wanted her back, a sentiment I could understand. Lena was a fine dog and a good companion.

The pup was a cute little ball of rust-colored fur, with a long tail, a mask of white on her face, and big eyes that seemed a bit sad. When Scot set her on the ground, she scampered a few steps and squatted. It was a pose we would see many times in weeks to come, as we tried to teach her to do her squatting in the field behind our house in town. After thinking several days about a name, we decided to call her Rosie.

Scot said that he'd had to make several calls to find a heeler pup with a full tail, one that wasn't "docked" (cut off). When he found one, he told the lady the pup would be replacing a dog we lost in the wildfires, and she gave it to him at no charge.

I'm sure that dog breeders have a good reason for docking the tail of a pup, but I don't know what it is and probably wouldn't be persuaded if I did. From my perspective (and Kris agreed), dogs need a tail. It adds to their vocabulary and expands the range of emotions that express their personality.

Knut and his men parked the little cabin on the site of my previous office, with the screen porch facing the south toward a rather spectacular view of the canyon wall rising 300 feet from the valley floor. They leveled it and installed metal skirting—and Knut never billed me for their time and labor.

The next day, I found a table and folding chair in the barn and moved them into the new office. I took a picture with my phone and sent it to family and friends, with the caption, "Back to work."

Actually, that prospect was a bit premature. It would be weeks before we got the office hooked up to water, plumbing, heat, and electricity, and the weather remained so cool, I had little desire to drive forty miles from town and spend four hours in a dark, cold place without a coffee pot.

But the building was there, waiting for me, and that was a big step forward.

When I got home that evening, Kris told me about her day in town. As usual on Wednesday, she went to the meeting of the Quilt Guild, but she was running late and walked in twenty minutes after it had started. She was surprised when the ladies turned and applauded. They had arranged for the meeting to be a shower for Kris, to replace some of the quilting tools and fabric she had lost in the fire, but they had kept it a secret.

One lady had driven all the way from Yukon, Oklahoma, and brought an envelope of cash donated by the ladies in her quilting group. Another lady, Lori Ganon, drove 120 miles from Amarillo. She and her husband owned and operated The Sewing Nook, a store for quilters. They replaced, free of charge, the sewing machine Kris had bought in their store and lost in the fire. Kris was overwhelmed by their kindness and generosity.

MAY 2017

We were fortunate to receive another dose of moisture at the end of April, even though it came in the form of wet snow, driven sideways by a savage north wind. Perryton and counties to the south got more rain than snow, but north of us in Oklahoma, Kansas, and southeast Colorado, it came as a freakish spring blizzard. I was astounded to hear that ten thousand cattle died in that storm. Most were in feedlots and drowned from snow blown into their lungs by the wind.

You add that pile of dead cattle to the ten thousand lost in the March fires and you get some sense of the risks involved in the ranching business.

May brought more rain. By May 5, I estimated that we had received 10 inches since January. (I had to estimate because all our rain gauges had melted in the fire.) Our pastures continued to green up and heal, and with all the old grass gone, the place took on the shine of a golf course. It was hard to believe that only a month before the land had been a desert of cinders and dirt.

I knew that some of that green came from ragweed and other plants that cattle won't eat, but the grass was looking good too, and our cows were going after it. I tried feeding cake every other day, then stopped altogether.

I still had a stockpile of grass hay, trucked in by generous people after the fire, but the cattle wouldn't touch it now, with all the fresh grass. It would remain stacked in the hay lot all summer, and by the time I started feeding again in November, it might be worthless for anything but garden compost.

This was an odd turn of events, going from having no hay to having a surplus of it, all in two months, and the story was the same across the three-state area that had been burned. Trucks were still pulling in to drop-off points in Canadian, Wheeler, Lipscomb, Beaver, and Ashland with round bales, but nobody needed them or had a place to store them.

I got a call from a trucker in Wheeler, saying that he was heading my way with a semi-load of good hay, and he wanted directions to the ranch. I urged him to please find someone around Wheeler who needed it, because I didn't. I never heard back from him, so he either unloaded the hay at the Wheeler drop-off or hauled it back to South Texas.

On May 8, Scot, Mark, Tina, and Kris went shopping for a double-wide modular home for the ranch. They found a nice one with 1,800 square feet and we bought it. None of us were excited about a modular home, but it provided us with the quickest way of getting back to something like a normal life on the ranch.

Scot trucked in heavy equipment and did the dirt work. He and his friends laid a water line and installed a septic system, and two days later the house was there on site—empty of furniture and not hooked up to electricity but on the ranch, with running water and two flush toilets. After living in our little duplex in town, I thought the home looked like a castle.

REANNA

On May 11, I had to leave the ranch and fly to a homeschool convention in Arlington, Texas. I did an evening program on Friday and signed books in our Maverick Books booth the rest of the time. Saturday afternoon, I caught a flight back to Amarillo, arriving around six.

Leaving the airport, I saw that our daughter, Ashley Wilson, had sent me a text, asking me to call her immediately.

In a trembling voice, she told me that her 13-year-old daughter, our granddaughter ReAnna, had been struck by a train in Canadian and killed. She had been walking to a store to buy Ashley a card for Mother's Day. Apparently she paused at the tracks, waiting for a westbound train to pass, then stepped into the path of an eastbound train she hadn't seen or heard. She was listening to music through earbuds attached to her cell phone.

It was shattering news, unthinkable. I was staggered and wondered how on earth I would break it to Kris. She was alone at the house in Perryton, where I wouldn't arrive for two hours. In that time, she might hear the news from someone else. I didn't want her to be alone when she did.

I called Sandra Splawn and told her what had happened. "Sandra, I hate to ask this, but would you and Ken go to the house and tell her? She needs someone to be there with her. She loved that little girl dearly, and this is going to be a terrible blow."

Sandra said of course they would. She called our pastor, Mark Metzger, and the three of them went to the house and gave Kris the news.

All the way home, I pictured ReAnna's crystal blue eyes and beautiful smile. The next morning, I went to Maverick Books and used my writing time to compose a few lines about this treasure of a girl.

Sunday morning, the sun rose as usual, sweeping away the darkness with clean golden light. After months of turbulent weather—an ice storm, wildfires, a blizzard, and a hail storm—we had a quiet, beautiful day. Spring had finally come to the Texas Panhandle.

That was my first thought when I looked out and saw the sunlight sparkling on green grass, but that thought was swept away by another: We won't be able to share it with ReAnna. I could hardly believe it.

If there was ever a spring flower, it was that little girl. She was sweet, smart, loyal, brave, and kind. She had been blessed with beautiful eyes and hair and a smile that would melt an iceberg. Her beauty came from an inner goodness that was as pure as an Easter lily. I'm sure she did something naughty in her short life, but I don't remember it.

She seemed to have no fear. Out at the ranch, she would do anything that came along. She fed cattle with me in the pickup and vaccinated calves at branding time.

Our two dogs adored her. If we drove off without them, they would follow until I stopped and let them ride in the cab with ReAnna.

She helped us pick wild plums in the summer, then made wild plum jelly with Kris. Kris taught her to sew and they made a quilt together.

She enjoyed singing with us in the living room on long winter evenings. I guess it never occurred to her that she couldn't play the mandolin, or that it might be hard, or that you're supposed to hire a teacher and take private lessons. Her grandmother played the mandolin, so she picked it up, learned three chords, and started playing "Silly Old Maid."

She started playing with us in the living room when we practiced, and the following Christmas we gave her a mandolin of her own. At home, she would close her bedroom door and play and sing. That became ReAnna's song, and when she sprouted up into a tall willow of a young lady, the words made a comic fit:

Old maid, skinny as a rail,
Blue jean queen with a pony tail.
You're just a daisy, not a rose
A country girl with a pointed nose.

In 2016, she went with us to the Texas Home School convention in Houston, sold books at our booth, and joined us onstage in singing our favorite song. She never showed any fear performing in front of an audience.

I had already decided that we would sing "Silly Old Maid" at her wedding, although I hadn't cleared it with her mother.

Stringing words together is my life's work, but I can't come up with words to explain why we had to lose ReAnna, just now as the charred hills are melting into green. It's too soon. Weren't we just getting started? I'm not ready to face a day without her.

We have to fall back on words written more than 2,500 years ago by an old man named Isaiah. "All men are like grass and all their glories are like the flowers of the field. The grass withers and the flowers fall, but the word of the Lord endureth forever."

I sent the piece to Ashley and Randy, hoping it might provide some comfort. They asked Mark Metzger, the pastor of our church in Perryton, to read it at the funeral in the Methodist church in Canadian.

The church was packed, with part of the crowd watching the service on a closed-circuit television in Fellowship Hall. The school had allowed students to attend, including ReAnna's teammates on the basketball team. They sat together as a group and cried when Cory Campbell read a touching eulogy. Entire families grieved the loss of ReAnna.

Alyssa Erickson, ReAnna's favorite cousin, had come with her mother from Amarillo. George Clay drove up from Bowie. Nikki came from San Antonio. Nathan and Missy Dahlstrom came from Lubbock with their three children. Tim Lambert and his daughter Stephanie also made the eight-hour round trip from Lubbock. Many friends from Perryton were there.

I had been scheduled to fly to College Station on Wednesday afternoon to do two Hank programs at the George H. W. Bush Presidential Library on Thursday. Gary Rinker had booked the engagement six months before, and the people at the library had arranged to bus in school children from communities in the College Station area. They had filled their 600-seat auditorium for both performances.

I consider myself a professional performer, and professionals show up for the job, but on Wednesday afternoon I had to be with Ashley and Randy at the funeral. Our family was carrying a heavy load of grief and needed to do our grieving together, with friends and the residents of Perryton and Canadian supporting and mourning with us.

I saw no way of keeping my commitment to the people at the Bush Library.

Gary Rinker mentioned this difficulty to a Perryton friend, Jason Schickedanz, who resolved it by offering to fly me down to College Station in his plane on Thursday morning. At 6:30, we lifted off the Perryton runway, buzzed the country home of Jason's dad, Larry, to make sure he wasn't loitering in his sheets, and headed for Central Texas.

The people at the library were grateful that I had come, and Jason and I made it back home in time for supper. Jason proved himself a true friend in a time of need, another quiet hero who stepped up when we really needed one.

For our family, the catastrophe of ReAnna's death came just as we were beginning to straighten our backs and recover from our losses in the fire. Stephen J. Pyne, a careful observer of mankind's relationship with fire, might have noted the irony that, after losing our home to "old fire," we lost ReAnna to "new fire," a diesel locomotive powered by an internal combustion engine of the Industrial Age.

In the days and weeks that followed, I tried to slip back into something close to a normal writing routine, now in my little office on the ranch. I got up in the mornings around 5:30 or 6, loaded my little pal Rosie into the pickup, and made the 45-minute commute to the ranch.

There, with Rosie chewing on a cardboard box or sleeping in my lap, I continued my work on this document about the fire. My office still didn't have water, but it was hooked up to electricity, so I had lights and an electric heater.

I couldn't stop thinking about ReAnna. Neither could Kris or Mark or Tina or Scot, and the grief of Ashley and Randy was beyond comprehension. My brother in Portland sent me an email, asking how we were doing. I wrote:

We don't know how we're doing: okay, not so good, sad, all of them.
We get up in the morning, pull on our clothes, and do something
besides pout, cry, and brood.
We're better off than anyone in Syria or Iraq.
I miss my home in the canyon. In the night, I think of ReAnna
stepping into the path of a hundred-ton locomotive.
I have many blessings, too much to give me license to complain.
I guess we're doing okay. Thanks.

ROSIE AND BRANDING

Rosie became a good companion during the days I spent alone on the ranch, thinking of ReAnna and the fire. The pup enjoyed riding with me to look at the grass and cattle and to check windmills and fence. I even coaxed her into riding in my lap on the lawn mower.

In *Story Craft*, I wrote a sentence I'm proud of: "Only the Maker of galaxies would have thought to give mankind such a marvelous gift as a dog." It's truly a miracle, this bond we have with dogs. It isn't as strong as the one between mother and child or husband and wife, but it's powerful.

I don't remember who said "I don't have enough faith to be an atheist," but it applies here. I don't have enough faith to believe that the bond we share with dogs arose through dumb luck or the random collision of molecules.

I was grateful for the gift of Rosie, and she will always have a special place in my heart.

On May 30, we held our spring branding. Mark was the roundup boss and assembled a crew of six able-bodied men, plus me. The younger guys did the riding, roping, and flanking. I would have preferred doing those jobs, and had done them with gusto in my prime, but now I took the old man's job of branding.

We had a beautiful spring day without extreme heat, high wind, or mosquitoes. At 2, we broke for lunch. Mark cooked steaks on the grill, Kris brought potato salad from town, Missy Dahlstrom and her daughters made a green salad, and we ate under the trees around the camper trailer.

The cattle were fat and sleek, and the ranch looked spectacular with green hills and canyons splashed with patches of red

Indian blanket wildflowers. If you didn't notice the charred skeletons of cedars and junipers, you wouldn't have been able to imagine how this place looked on March 7—like a scene from a World War I battlefield.

On branding day, the cowboys killed a rattlesnake near the barn and saw another that escaped into a hole. That same afternoon, two of our ranch neighbors reported killing four rattlers. The next day, Daisy turned up with a snakebite on her left hind leg. It looked bad enough that Kris took her to the vet in Perryton.

When I picked her up two days later, Dr. Randy Skaggs said that he had treated three snakebite cases that week, an unusually high number. He speculated that the wildfires had disrupted something in the snakes' normal patterns and that this was likely to be a bad season for snakebites.

My guess was that the fires killed a lot of field mice and rats, and the snakes were coming out of their usual hiding places and hunting where mice had survived, around buildings and piles of scrap metal.

Whatever the cause, it wasn't good news. Daisy had a powerful nose and could sniff out any snake that came into her territory. She had established herself as a deadly enemy of garter snakes, bull snakes, and hognose snakes. These were harmless creatures, good snakes, and I always tried to protect them, but Daisy was determined to kill them.

In past years, she had alerted us to rattlesnakes around the house, but I had never known her to attack one. I worried that her success with the lightweights would draw her into combat with a rattler that could do her serious damage.

The fact that she had been bitten on the back leg, not the face, suggested that it might have been an ambush, not a fight, which gave me some hope that she might have a sensible fear of rattlesnakes. If not, at least she had acquired some immunity to future bites, in case she couldn't restrain herself from rushing into battle.

Daisy recovered from the bite and we brought her back to the ranch, but I was concerned about Rosie. She had all the innocence and curiosity that make pups adorable but vulnerable to things that strike and inject poison. I took her to the vet and got her vaccinated for rattlesnake venom. I couldn't bear the thought of losing her.

JUNE 2017

Our country had made a remarkable recovery from the fire, but we weren't sure how much of it was cosmetic and temporary. The time was approaching when Mark and I had to make a decision on whether or not our 5,700 acres of post-burn pasture could support sixty-six cows and calves. Range experts were cautioning producers about stocking pastures too heavily too soon, and we didn't want to hurt our grass.

I sought advice from Hemphill County agent Andy Holloway and Eddy Corse from the Roberts County office of the NRCS (Natural Resources Conservation Service). Both were kind enough to come out to the ranch and look at our country. They were impressed with the condition of our grasses and noted that the buffalo and grama were already making seed.

They were also pleased with the kill we'd gotten on juniper, cactus, and yucca. They predicted that with decent rains, the ranch would be in great shape by fall, and agreed with me and Mark that the fire had done our country a world of good.

They thought the ranch could run our cows over the summer, if we rotated them from pasture to pasture, but they also felt that a complete rest would give the grass a chance to seed out and root down. Eddy told me about a program NRCS was offering to defer grazing on burned land until November. I wasn't keen on asking a government agency for help, but the longer I thought about it, the better it sounded. I called George Chapman and asked his opinion, and he didn't hesitate.

"Take it! It's the best thing you could do. I went through this when our ranch burned in 2006. The grass comes back and looks great, but it needs a rest. Give that country some time to heal up. Bring your cows over here and we'll look after them during the summer. Take 'em back home in November and wean the calves. Perfect."

I also made contact with some range management people at Texas Tech University and offered to let them use the ranch as a research location to study the effects of the March fire. On the morning of June 12, I met Dr. Ron Sosebee and Dr. Carlos Villalobos at the ranch and gave them a tour.

We visited the two springs in Pickett Canyon, Moonshine Springs and Scott Springs. When we bought the ranch in 1990, neither of those springs was active, but the presence of big cedar trees and a few cottonwoods told us that water was not far below the surface. It appeared to me that during the droughts of the Thirties and Fifties, silt had washed down from the top country and buried the springs. Springs don't have enough head pressure to break through the silt, but if you dig a channel, water will flow.

The kids and I found several moss-covered rocks and dug around them with shovels, releasing a trickle of water that we channeled into little pools. In our dry country, that was cause for celebration. A few years later, Scot made a deal with his friend Sean Dooley to clean out the creek bed with a big "long stick" trackhoe. He removed about three feet of dirt until he reached the rocky surface of the original streambed, giving each spring several hundred feet of flowing water and pools.

The 2017 fire brought major changes to the springs, killing all the big cedar trees and a few cottonwoods that had endured there competing for water and sunlight with the cedars. I was sad to see that a cottonwood I had planted at Scott Springs fifteen years before didn't survive. It was a two-foot sprout when I transplanted it on the edge of the water and it had grown into a graceful thirty-foot tree. The fire had left it a black dead pole.

But we noticed something else. A number of little cottonwood sprouts had popped up from the tree's root system, so while we had lost one big cottonwood, we were getting twenty little ones in return. The fire had created a much friendlier environment for the cottonwoods, which don't compete well against cedars. Cedars create a canopy of shade that kills the ground around it, and they pull a large amount of water from the springs.

The Texas Tech guys pointed out that ash from the fire had brought nutrients into the soil and the cottonwoods were responding to it. In ten years, we might have so many cottonwoods growing at those springs we will have to cull them down.

While we were driving around the ranch, we noticed swarms of big insects that we call cedar flies. They are five times the size of a housefly and are a source of torment to horses. We've always had them in the canyons during the summer months, but I had never seen so many of them. I wondered if the fires had altered their normal patterns. If cedar flies live in cedar trees, there was no question that the fire had reshuffled the cards.

HOUSEKEEPING AT THE RANCH

During the first weeks of June, we continued the slow process of getting our new double-wide house ready for occupation. We were making progress, but our lives were scattered over a sprawl of four structures that were incomplete:

Kris continued making the town house livable, but it wasn't home.

The move-in house at the ranch had water but no electricity and little furniture.

My office at the ranch had electricity but no water.

The camper trailer at the ranch had water and electricity but developed a mysterious leak, so we had to shut off the water and I had to rent a portable latrine.

But Scot kept things moving on the double-wide house. Under his watchful eye, workers hooked up the electricity, water, and septic system, put skirting around the perimeter, installed the air conditioning unit, and delivered a washer, dryer, and deep freezer.

Mark attended an estate sale in Amarillo and snapped up tables, chairs, and lamps at a bargain price. We rented a covered trailer and hauled them to the ranch. Kris went shopping for beds, sheets, a sofa and chair, bar stools, coffee maker, microwave oven, and something I wouldn't have thought about: forty light bulbs. New double-wides don't come with light bulbs.

Our church in Perryton threw a housewarming party to replace the kitchen and household items we had lost. Once again, we were overwhelmed by the generosity of the people in our community.

On Friday, June 16, we decided to spend our first night at the ranch, even though most of our clothes and miscellaneous items remained in town. You have to start somewhere.

Kris's brother, Scot Dykema, had come for a weekend visit and we stayed at the ranch. The house proved to be surprisingly comfortable. We cooked steaks and roasting ears on

Mark's propane grill and ate outside on a picnic table, enjoying a lovely, calm summer evening on the ranch.

We had no porch, yard, grass, trees, or sidewalks, but we had a house that was warm, dry, and comfortable. It was good to be back where we belonged.

GOODBYE TO THE COWS

Toward the end of June, Nathan Dahlstrom, Mark, and I gathered all the cattle on the ranch, separated the cows and calves, and loaded the animals onto three trucks that hauled them 120 miles west to George Chapman's ranch north of Amarillo. Even though our country was looking good and appeared to be recovering well from the fire, we would give it a season to rest and make seed.

The ranch fell into an odd silence when the cattle had gone. I enjoyed caring for livestock and participating in their simple rhythms. It's something humans have been doing for at least five thousand years, maybe longer, and I think it's a relationship that gives depth and perspective to human endeavors.

The cattle and I sometimes had different opinions about where they should be and what they should be doing (I called it "ranch management"), but we had always worked through our differences. I gave them free room and board, clean water, salt blocks, and grass, and they gave me an honest job, good lean grass-fed beef, some income, and a certain amount of stoic companionship.

Cows don't talk, hold political opinions, or stare at cell phones, and that can be refreshing. I don't assume they like me, but sometimes I get the impression that they do. We had suffered together through down cattle markets, a serious drought, ice storms, and the fire of March 6, and when the trucks roared away, I missed them.

CHAPTER 4

Eight Months After the Fire

BY NOVEMBER, I WAS SETTLED into my new office, which had electric heat, electric lights, running water, inside plumbing, and a coffee pot. Mark had bought me a 3' x 7' bookshelf and we set it up on the north wall. It was tiny, compared to the shelves in my old office, but adequate, since I had very few books that needed shelving.

But that was changing. I had begun buying books about fire and fire ecology and replacing some of the hundreds of books I had lost: several translations of the Bible, books by John Graves and J. Evetts Haley, books on ancient Egypt, and new copies of my own books, the ones I had written.

Generous people, some of whom I didn't even know, had sent books by Ben K. Green, J. Frank Dobie, Elmer Kelton, and other Texas authors. Three people gave me first edition copies of my first book, *Through Time and the Valley*.

I had even acquired a box of books and articles on Southern Plains archeology, gathered up by friends in the Panhandle archeology community, primarily Doug Wilkens, Doug Boyd, Rolla Shaller, and the family of the late Jim Couzzourt.

I never dreamed I would find replacements for the scholarly work of Chris Lintz, Richard Drass, Brett Cruse, Jack Hughes, David Hughes, Jack Hoffman, Robert Brooks, Douglas Owsley, Scott Brosowske, and Doug Boyd. Those books had a small circulation, mostly among professionals in the field, and were very hard to find.

Kris and I had settled into our double-wide home on the ranch. It wasn't as big or elaborate as the house we'd lost, but it was comfortable and we were thankful to have it. Bit by bit we were filling in the blanks of things we had lost—furniture, bedding, and household items. With winter coming on, our thoughts were turning to warm clothes, gloves, snow boots, and wool blankets.

Our closets were not nearly as full as before, but we found some comfort in that shift. We didn't need as many things as we did before, or thought we did.

We were playing music again, Kris with the Nugget mandolin we had carried out of the house on March 6 and I with the new Stelling Staghorn banjo I had ordered back in April. Geoff Stelling shipped it to me in September from his shop in Virginia, and it was a great instrument, even better than the two I had lost in the fire.

At my request, Geoff had decorated the peghead with a delicate inlay cut from a piece of mother of pearl, the face of Hank the Cowdog. It was a fitting tribute to the dog who had made our ranch payments for many years.

Workers from Diamond M Construction in Gruver had begun building a cedar porch on the front of the double-wide. That was one of the things we missed most when we lost our home: the big porch where we had spent many pleasant hours with cowboys, kinfolk, archeologists, and visitors from distant places.

Kris had set up one room in the new house for her quilting, and most of the new fabric and equipment came from donations by quilters in Perryton, Canadian, and Amarillo. They understood the loss she had suffered, as only quilters can. Kris returned to making beautiful designs out of cloth and thread and tried not to think about the ten quilts she had lost in the fire.

Of course she could never forget the little girl she had been teaching to quilt, ReAnna. It was an ache that never went away. We thought of her every day and prayed every day for her parents.

Kris was looking at house plans prepared by architect Ryan Wilkens, Doug and Cara's son, and was starting to think about rebuilding on the site of the house we had lost, but it was a difficult process. Kris and I often wondered if we had the energy or the will to start over. When you get bucked off hard at the age of forty, you climb back on, but at seventy-three, you wonder if it's worth the effort.

Mark and Scot kept the process moving and helped in every way they could. It was important to them that we rebuild and get back to where we were, whole and restored, or as close to that as we could get.

If we did rebuild, we would pay close attention to fireproof materials on the exterior. When we had built the original house in 1993, we weren't thinking of that at all. How things had changed!

Cold weather reminded me that the time was approaching for us to do something with the cattle we had moved to George Chapman's place north of Amarillo. We had calves to wean and yearlings to sell, and then we needed to decide what to do with the cows.

Some ranchers and livestock scholars advised producers to sell all breeding animals that had gone through a bad fire, even if they didn't show immediate signs of damage. Injury to lungs, hooves, and other organs might not show up for a year or two, and holding those animals could prove to be more expensive in the long run than clearing the herd and starting all over with young heifers.

That was a tough call, but we ended up keeping them. George ran them through the winter and never sent us a bill for pasture lease.

THE PASTURES

As for the ranch itself, it appeared that most of the junipers exposed to the fire were killed, which we celebrated in the name of brush control. The prairie would be much better without them, and the next time we had a fire, it would have a lot less fuel, especially in Pickett Canyon where we hoped to rebuild our home.

We got a good kill on broomweed, prickly pear cactus, and yucca. Some of it would come back, but maybe before it got a good hold the native grasses would take root and reclaim some of the ground.

It was hard to judge how the grass had fared, but what I saw looked good. We were fortunate to receive above average rainfall over the summer, which seems to be the most crucial element in grass recovery, and of course we had moved the cattle off the ranch and given the grass a season of rest. I noticed more tall grasses than usual in the fall: Indian grass, little bluestem, sideoats grama, and big bluestem.

On the downside, ragweed seemed to have prospered after the fire, moving into every bare spot. However, county agents and USDA staff pointed out that, after a fire, ragweed wasn't a bad thing to have around, much preferable to naked ground. Ragweed shades the ground and inhibits a buildup of heat. It anchors the soil, prevents wind and water erosion, and provides feed for birds. It will hold a blowing snow and allow moisture to percolate into the ground.

I was definitely interested in learning more about prescribed burning but was also aware that our terrain would make it difficult. On the flats north of us, plowing, mowing, or grading fireguards wouldn't be much of a problem, but that was not the case in our canyons. Some parts of the ranch were not accessible to spray rigs or heavy equipment.

Before the fire, we had a good population of wild turkey and an exceptional crop of bobwhite quail. After the fire, I saw very few of either and no rabbits, either cottontails or jackrabbits. Maybe the fire had changed their habitat to such an extent that they moved out, or maybe they had suffered a heavy death loss.

For twenty-seven years, a colony of buzzards had roosted in a big cottonwood tree near my office in Pickett Canyon. The fire killed their roosting tree and the buzzards moved out. I never thought I would miss a colony of buzzards, but I did. I'm glad to report that they came back the following spring and have decided to stay.

WATER EROSION

Another change I noticed in the months after the fire had to do with the most precious commodity on any ranch on the Southern Plains: water. In June, we had a hard two-inch rain that, I was surprised to find, filled a pond in Pickett Canyon. It backed up water into a small barn and flooded our picnic ground to the extent that picnic tables and wooden benches were floating around in the pond, surrounded by a quantity of charred wood that had washed out of the canyon.

In the twenty-seven years we had owned the ranch, the pond had filled only twice, and it had taken a five-inch rain to do it. In the summer of 2017, it filled and overflowed twice, with nothing close to a five-inch downpour.

This suggested that the fire had altered something in the watershed, perhaps hardening the soil surface, making it less able to hold and absorb rainwater. Further, my guess was that, before the fire, dead grass and brush had slowed the movement of runoff water, and the fire destroyed all those little dams.

As a result, our ranch roads washed badly over the summer, so that Roberts County, the oil companies, and I had to devote considerable tractor time to keeping them in shape for vehicle traffic. One road going up the caprock east of headquarters washed out four times. Another road that led up to Hodges Mesa acquired a gash six feet deep.

On the positive side, the runoff water filled two ponds in the east pasture that had gone dry in the drought of 2011–2014, killing all our fish. Now the ponds had returned and were as full as they could get. With any luck, we will have some good fishing in a few years, as we did when Mark was a boy and living at home.

SPRINGS

Another change I observed was the effect the fire had on seep springs. I had read and heard that when fire kills off invader trees, springs usually become more active. Each cedar or juniper pulls 30–40 gallons of water from the soil every day, and when you multiply that times thousands of trees, it becomes a considerable amount.

I had expected to see an increase in spring activity and over the summer made frequent trips to the three active springs on our ranch: Scott Springs and Moonshine Springs in Pickett

Canyon and Indian Springs in west pasture. These were not large springs, just a series of foot-deep pools that extended twenty or thirty yards, but they were big enough to provide water for livestock and wildlife. On a hot day, a thirsty cowboy could get a drink from them.

During Prohibition, every seep spring on the ranch provided water for a moonshine still. Mark and I had located the remains of seven stills.

It appeared that Moonshine Springs had increased its flow, but I couldn't see that Indian Springs or Scott Springs had changed much. I was disappointed. But one day in November, I noticed wet ground where the road crossed Pickett Creek. That was strange. I glanced upstream and saw a small pool of water in a spot where we had never seen one, two hundred yards south of Moonshine Springs. Maybe there were more pools.

The creek bed in this part of the canyon was obscured by a heavy growth of grass and ragweed, as well as the blackened remains of burned trees, so I couldn't get a good look at it from the pasture trail. I walked down the dry streambed and saw mud, then a puddle of ash-colored water, then a nice little pool. Actually, the dogs found it and I heard them splashing around. It was deep enough so that they had to swim.

I had discovered fifty yards of spring pools that were producing more surface water than Moonshine and Scott Springs ever had, and in a spot where we had never expected to find live water.

To say I was thrilled would be an understatement. Maybe you have to be a rancher to understand the joy of finding water in this arid land. Water is LIFE! It brings sub-irrigated grasses, water-loving trees (willows and cottonwoods), birds, deer, frogs—and the animals that hunt them.

I took pictures with my phone and texted them to Mark and Scot, and they were excited too. As boys, they had worked beside me with shovels to revive Scott and Moonshine Springs, so they understood the thrill of discovering water.

Several days passed before it occurred to me that I should check the next canyon to the west, Big Rocks. In all the years we had owned the ranch, we had never found even a damp spot in this deep majestic canyon. What I encountered astonished me: 200 yards of spring pools, some of them two to three feet deep, producing even more standing water than I had found days before in Pickett Canyon.

I assumed that the appearance of all these spring pools was a direct result of the fire. Keith Blair, a burn specialist in Lubbock, told me that he conducts regular prescribed burns for a customer in the Texas Hill Country, and the main objective of the burns is to increase spring activity by ridding the property of juniper. Our fire in March had accomplished that on a grand scale, killing much of the cedar and juniper not only in our canyons but for miles around in all directions.

It was possible that these were cool-weather springs that would vanish in the summer, then appear again in the fall, but several of those pools had cattails growing in them, an indication that the water had been there for several months. The springs had popped up in the summer and we hadn't noticed them.

As we approached the Thanksgiving holidays, my assessment of things was mostly positive. Our cattle had survived. The fire had improved range conditions on the ranch and revived our springs. The pastures had enjoyed a good growing season and had received a rest.

Kris and I had set up housekeeping on the ranch and were reestablishing some of the comfortable patterns of our life before the fire. The double-wide house lacked the space to accommodate our traditional family gathering at Thanksgiving, so we spent the holiday with our children and grandchildren at Scot and Tina's lovely home southeast of Amarillo, on the rim of Palo Duro Canyon.

On Thanksgiving Day, we had much to be thankful for.

CHAPTER 5

*The First Anniversary of the Fire**

AS WE MOVED INTO WINTER, I began hearing rumblings about dry weather that was having an adverse effect on fields planted to winter wheat. This came as a surprise. How could we be dry again? We had just come through an unusually wet summer. Our ponds were full and our grass had made a spectacular recovery from the fire.

But after several good rains in September, our moisture stopped, and in our region it doesn't take long to go from mud to blowing dust. That is one of the prominent features of the Panhandle and South Plains and one of the reasons this area was the last in Texas to be settled by farmers and ranchers who had to make a living from the soil.

---

* Portions of this chapter appeared as a *World* magazine Digital Saturday Series essay, March 17, 2018. https://world.wng.org/content/smelling_for_smoke

But surely we wouldn't have to start worrying about fires again in the spring, would we?

October, November, and December came and went, bone dry, the driest anyone could remember. Weather forecasters were predicting a return of La Niña in 2018, which usually brings lower precipitation to our area. All at once, tall grass and dry weather were bringing back memories of the conditions we had seen in March 2017.

Sure enough, in December we began hearing reports of grass fires in counties to the west of us: Oldham, Potter, Carson, Hutchinson, and Gray. These were not huge fires, but they highlighted what fire experts had been saying for years: for whatever reason, fire was becoming a fact of life in our region and it wasn't likely to go away anytime soon. February brought more reports of fires.

On Friday, March 2, 2018, almost a year after our big fire, I went to my writing office at the usual time and checked the weather report on my computer. The National Weather Service had issued a Red Flag Fire Watch for Sunday, March 4, for the entire Texas Panhandle.

On Saturday, the watch was upgraded to a warning: high temperatures (75), strong winds (35–40 mph with higher gusts), and low humidity. A map on the website of the National Oceanic and Atmospheric Administration (NOAA) showed the "critical" area stretching all the way from El Paso, Texas, up into Colorado and Nebraska.

This forecast brought a creepy echo of the warnings we'd gotten three days before the 2017 fire, and it came almost a year to the day after that event. Would we be observing the one-year anniversary of our fire with another fire that might destroy everything we had replaced and rebuilt since that day?

It seemed almost too cruel to imagine. Kris and Mark were working on house plans. We had just begun to use and enjoy the nice cedar porch on the front of our double-wide. Scot and Tina had given us a barbecue grill so that we could cook outside. We had chairs and a little table on the porch.

We had replaced some of the clothes we had lost, some of the books and DVDs, boots and hats, pots and pans, furniture, beds, towels, reading lamps, silverware, plates, can openers, fingernail clippers, Kris's sewing machine . . . on and on and on.

And now we had to think about losing them again?

The wind blew hard Friday and Saturday, and we were on high alert. A few fires broke out around Fritch, Dumas, and Amarillo, but they weren't large or close to us, and firefighters got them under control. It appeared that the worst day would come on Sunday, so Kris and I began discussing plans, in case we had to evacuate . . . again.

At dawn on Sunday, the wind was calm. A layer of thin clouds covered the sky, and I could smell dampness in the air. It didn't have the feel of a bad fire day, but NOAA's National Weather Service Prediction Center foresaw something else:

> A compact belt of 80 to 90-knot mid-level winds— near the base of a large-scale western US trough— will move eastward over the four corners region and emerge over the plains through tonight. As this occurs, a lee cyclone over eastern Colorado is expected to rapidly deepen to ~996 mb while shifting toward western Kansas/Nebraska by evening. An associated dryline will extend southward from the surface cyclone—initially being located along a N/S line near the Colorado/Kansas and Texas/New Mexico borders this morning before surging eastward into western Nebraska, western Kansas, most of the Oklahoma/Texas Panhandles, and western

portions of the Edwards Plateau into this evening. A cold front is then forecast to shift across much of the central and southern High Plains tonight.

The language of meteorology had always been opaque to me, but I understood the bottom line: this was likely to be a bad day on the Southern Plains, and the "critical" area covered 238,000 square miles. There were a lot of ranch homes, trailer houses, and double-wides in that expanse of prairie, and Kris and I lived in one of them.

It was hard for me to judge how vulnerable we might be this time. The 2017 fire had killed thousands of cedar trees and destroyed their canopy of sappy, flammable foliage, but it had left blackened trunks and limbs that could, under the right conditions, make a big fire. The "right conditions" would include enough tall grass and enough wind to ignite a tree trunk.

We had a lot of tall grass and a lot of dead trees, and the NWS was predicting strong winds.

Kris and I talked it over and decided that she would go to church and stay the night in town. I would join her in the after-noon—possibly running from a fire. She began the forty-mile drive to town in her Explorer, loaded with boxes of clothes, family pictures, and the quilt she was working on. For the past several weeks, we had made it a practice to carry our musical instruments, laptops, and charger cords any time we left home.

Staying at the ranch on a Red Flag fire day involved a cer-tain amount of risk and was probably pointless, but this was my home and I didn't want to leave. I had two dogs to keep me company: Daisy the yellow Lab, and Rosie the red heeler who had been my loyal companion since the 2017 fire.

If a fire appeared to be heading our way, I would start two sprinklers to wet down the south and west sides of the house.

We had a buffer of bare ground around the double-wide and had installed a metal roof for this kind of situation. In a firestorm, a metal roof offers some protection from flying embers.

But I worried about my writing office, a 12' x 30' trailer house with log veneer siding that gave it the rustic look of a cabin. It also had a buffer of bare ground and mowed weeds around it, and a metal roof, but I was concerned about the wood siding, which had gotten very dry over the past five months. A hot fire might ignite the siding, even if the flames never reached the structure.

I hooked up the water trailer to my pickup and began filling the 500-gallon fiberglass tank. While it filled, I moved a computer, some tax records, vehicle titles, and checkbooks from my office to a metal barn, then moved some boxes from the house, things Kris had packed up that morning: coats, boots, dresses, her sewing machine, and other items she had shopped for and bought in the months after the 2017 fire.

The thought of having to go through that ordeal again was depressing to both of us, but especially to Kris. She had told me, "Since you never shop, you have *no idea*."

I spent an hour spraying water on the wood exterior of my office, then wetting down the grass around our diesel generator. A month after the fire, George Chapman had hauled it to Amarillo and found several mechanics who thought they could rebuild it, even though it looked like a total loss. They succeeded, and now it was back on the ranch.

The 2017 fire destroyed hundreds of utility poles and miles of power lines; it took crews a week to restore service to rural customers. Our new modular home was all-electric, so when the power went out, we had no lights, heat, or water. The house became a dead shell, which underscored the importance of protecting the generator from fire.

Several times in the afternoon, Rosie and I drove the Ranger to a high spot above the canyon and checked the horizon. I feared we would see smoke, but we didn't.

Back at the house, I tried to read *Biblical Archeology Review* but found myself making frequent trips to the porch to look for smoke. At five o'clock, the wind began to diminish. I called Kris and told her that I intended to stay the night at the ranch.

I cooked a modest supper and watched a movie, frequently checking for smoke. At 9:30, I retired with a book and opened a window in the bedroom. If I awoke and smelled smoke, I would load two bags, two dogs, and one banjo into the pickup and head for town.

I don't know whether the smell of smoke would have pulled me out of sleep or not, but I awoke at 6 a.m. to find the house still standing. The dogs and I had made it through the night.

Monday brought more high wind, this time out of the north, and we remained under a critical Red Flag Warning. I sprayed more water on my office and spent another day checking for smoke. The dogs and I stayed at the ranch that night and awoke to face still another day of fire danger, this one being March 6, our fire anniversary.

A few friends remembered the occasion and called or sent text messages. It was an ugly, cold, somber day, filled with sad ghosts of memory. I sprayed water and checked for smoke. At three o'clock the wind speed reached 29 mph and the relative humidity dropped to 10 percent, but we had no fires.

Around 6 that evening, the wind slacked off and Kris returned to the ranch. With her there, the house became a home again. We celebrated our fire anniversary with a glass of wine.

Those three days of waiting for catastrophe seemed a fog. Nothing had felt right or comfortable. You're tempted to call someone, but who? And what would you say—*I'm remembering last year and it's sad and scary?* So you fret and pace and indulge in flights of self-pity. "Why me, Lord? Wasn't one burnout enough? Our friends are weary of worrying about John and Kris. Last March, they donated food, clothes, furniture, hay, kitchen supplies, fencing material, and money. They're tired of helping us, and we're tired of needing help."

But then you step into the light of perspective. Shirley Cooper, a member of our church, died Sunday night while I was alone on the ranch, on edge and feeling sorry for myself. She was an outstanding teacher, a dignified, beautiful woman, the mother of two children, and Don's wife for more than half a century.

She had lived with cancer for fifteen years, with all the pain, indignity, fear, and discouragement that comes with cancer treatments and interminable trips to Houston and Amarillo. There were dozens of people like her in our town who suffered mostly in silence, true heroes whose stories we rarely heard except in bits and pieces.

Put in that context, what did I have to complain about?

Our fire anniversary came and went, but the fire danger stayed with us. The drought deepened, with April bringing day after day of strong winds. The Red Flag Warnings that had caused us so much anxiety in March became common-place. We had heard them so many times, we ceased to flinch at or even notice them.

Every day brought reports about new fires that had bro-ken out, old fires that had reignited with a change in wind direction, heroic efforts by volunteer firefighters, and fund-raising projects to help local fire departments replace broken equipment.

In mid-April, a series of fires in western Oklahoma burned 400,000 acres, and calls went out for donations of hay for our Oklahoma neighbors who had lost all their pastures. I contacted the OSU Extension Service and offered to donate a truckload of hay that had come to us under the same circumstances in 2017. It wasn't the best of hay, having gone through a summer of exposure to rain and sunlight, but hay was in short supply and somebody's cows would prefer moldy hay to dirt and cinders.

The pattern of dry, windy weather continued into May. Occasional afternoon storms popped up, and we managed to snag a few rains of half an inch or less that might have decreased the fire hazard. But the Red Flag Warnings continued, and firefighters responded almost daily to fires in the western Panhandle and eastern New Mexico. One fire in Armstrong County, southwest of us, burned for ten days and covered 75,000 acres.

We remained vigilant until May 23, when the eastern Panhandle received its first good general rain in seven months. At the ranch, we got an inch and a half and felt a huge sense of relief. We continued receiving rains in June. At last, we had made it through the fire season of 2018.

It was around this time that Mark sent us a song he had written and recorded with his band, Comanche Moon. It was about the fire . . . and it was beautiful.

Restoration*

The night was empty on the highway, all the world was quiet,
Everything seemed alright.
'Til strokes of orange ripped across the night at the valley's edge,
The devil was dancing there.
He whipped and twirled across the sagebrush hills,
And like a child, I watched him go.
I didn't know that he was dancing inside your home.
When morning broke upon the ashes in the gray light dawn,
The smoke was still rising up.
And I dropped the curtain with some racing words on your old
      routines
And every familiar thing.
With words of Job still running through your mind
You lift your eyes and face the sun.
It can burn you out, but don't let it bring you down.
The King and Queen have lost their castle and there's no peace in
      the land
Until they return again.
And April showers, like forgiveness, on the prairie
Turn all the black to green.
You'd rather work your hands than ask a favor.
To you, it seemed easier that way.
You said, "Look, my son, the hard times will make you strong."
Your road leads further back than forward and it's hard, I know,
To work up the will to hope.
But if restoration is a burden that's too heavy,
Let me be your strength.
The months turn into seasons three by four,

---

*   Written by Mark Erickson; performed and recorded by Comanche
Moon on their album *Country Music Deathstar*.

Seasons roll on into years,
And I can't wait to see what good will come from it all.
When the rain comes and life returns
And the seasons bring restoration
This present darkness will become
A distant memory, just like the bad dreams
That you dream at night that dissipate with the morning light.

CHAPTER 6

The Second Anniversary of the Fire

THE WEATHER ON MARCH 6, 2019—the second anniversary of the fire—turned out to be quite different from that of the year before, when we spent months on high alert. The air was soft and still when Rosie and I left the house in the dark and drove a mile north to my writing office. It even carried a hint of moisture.

At the office, Rosie sprang up on the cot that served as her Official Spot during my writing time, completed her ritual of turning around three times, dropped into the shape of a C, and closed her eyes. I opened my laptop and checked the weather. I was relieved to find a good report: 53 percent humidity, 10 mph wind, and no red banner across the top bearing the dreaded words "RED FLAG FIRE WARNING."

I checked my email and saw that Mark had forwarded a message he had posted on his Facebook page:

On this day 183 years ago, the Alamo fell. On this day two years ago, my family's home where I grew up and where my parents still lived burned down in one of the largest wildfires in modern Texas history. We didn't lose as much as some, but ours was a loss.

Two years later, my brother Scot and his crew are underway rebuilding a new house right on the ashes of the old one. We both have encouraged, nudged, perhaps at times pushed our parents to take on the challenge of rebuilding. It would have been easier to stay down, but that's not how we roll. We're going to win!

The post included pictures Mark had taken the morning after the fire, when he had been the first to see the ruins. The pictures brought back a flood of memories.

After putting in my time at the office, I drove to the house site. Scot and his crew of three men had brought heavy equipment from Amarillo the day before and were well into the task of moving dirt to build a pad for the new house. They had two track loaders, a Cat motor grader, and a dirt packer.

I got out of the pickup and watched. In the grader, one of Scot's employees skinned off six inches of loose dirt and created a surface behind him that resembled a cabinet top. Scot was operating one of the loaders, moving dirt for the grader to level. I couldn't see my son's face through the tinted window but recognized the signature pattern of his work: fast and precise.

I hadn't expected him to stop his machine when he saw me (he was very serious when it came to dirt work) but he did. The door flew open and he jumped to the ground. Rosie recognized him, dashed out, and leaped up on his leg. He rubbed her ears and greeted her, then asked me, "What do you think?"

"I don't know how you can level a space this big."

"You'd be surprised what you can do with a million dollars' worth of equipment. Robert has a laser. That helps."

"Do you know that today is the second anniversary of the fire?"

He hosed me with a flat stare. "Of course. That's why we're here. It's time to get you back in your house."

Rebuilding our home had been a long process, but it appeared that we were finally moving in that direction.

Our second fire anniversary came and went without the kind of anxiety we had experienced in 2018. A few grassfires broke out in counties west of us, but they didn't amount to much. We weren't as dry as we had been in 2018 and, most important, we were spared the kind of brutal winds that drove the big fires of 2017.

Five days later, on March 11, a major weather system moved into the Panhandle. Light rain began in the night and continued, off and on, over the next twenty-four hours. When I went out in the dark on Wednesday morning, I checked the rain gauge in the beam of my headlights and saw 1.75 inches in the tube. What a welcome sight! I sent out messages to friends and kinfolk that we had gotten the best fire insurance money could buy.

But forecasters were warning of high winds on the backside of the system that had brought the rain. It was a powerful system that created something I had never heard of, a "bomb cyclone," caused by a sudden drop in barometric pressure. By eleven o'clock, the southwest wind was howling at 30–40 miles per hour, with higher gusts.

I was feeding cattle when the empty paper feed sacks began flying out of the back of my pickup. The wind tore the wool cap off my head and made the simple act of walking difficult. I had trouble opening the door of my pickup; it occurred to me that such a wind could jerk a pickup door right off its hinges.

The wind blew harder in the afternoon, gusting up into the range of 70 to 80 miles per hour. The Amarillo airport cancelled flights, trees toppled, semi-trucks blew onto their sides, and a train was blown off the tracks near Logan, New Mexico.

We didn't lose electrical service at the ranch but 121,000 customers in Texas and eastern New Mexico did, including those in the nearby towns of Spearman, Gruver, and Canadian. In states north of us, Colorado and Nebraska, the storm became a screaming blizzard that stranded hundreds of motorists on highways.

I stayed inside that afternoon and didn't worry about fires, assuming that the rain had made us immune. Not quite. Around 2:30, two utility poles blew down on a ranch north of Miami and started a grassfire about twenty miles due south of us. It was on a trajectory that could have taken it to Canadian (which had already lost its electricity), and first responders were preparing for the worst. But late in the afternoon the wind swung around to the northwest and sent the flames into a canyon where it burned itself out. It burned "only" 2,500 acres.

One trembles at the thought of what that fire might have done and how far it might have gone if we hadn't gotten the rain and if the wind hadn't shifted. It raised the unnerving possibility that in such a high wind, there is no such thing as immunity to fire. Fire can cut steel when an acetylene torch feeds oxygen to a flame, so maybe a fire in front of a sixty mile per hour wind will burn anything in its path, no matter how moist it is.

Many of us in the Panhandle were wondering, "Have we always had these fierce winds in March or is this something new?" I have vivid memories of dust storms during the drought of the Fifties when street lamps came on in the middle of the day and the light bulb on the ceiling of my fifth-grade class had a halo of dust around it.

We had wind and dust back then, but I don't recall that anyone felt the dread of fire that entered our experience in March 2006.

A CHANGING OF THE GUARD

In May, Rosie and I drove up into Pickett Canyon and conducted a walking survey of the area around Moonshine Springs. Before the fire, it had been the location of one of the most striking features on our ranch: a rare untouched forest of eastern red cedar trees.

The 2017 blaze went through those stately trees like a Sherman tank through a chicken house, leaving a scene of total destruction: hundreds of stark blackened poles standing over stark blackened soil. I have been told that redberry cedar will resprout from its roots, but our eastern red cedar and one-seed juniper did not. They were graveyard dead, and through the summer and fall of 2017, nothing grew beneath the charred tombstones.

In 2018, the bare ground beneath the dead cedars finally returned to life and produced a solid carpet of ragweed, apparently the only species that could thrive in the baked ashy soil. Here and there a few brave sprigs of soapberry popped up, but not many.

What I found in May 2019 surprised me. I had expected to see another thick crop of ragweed on what used to be the floor of the cedar forest. Because ragweed produces an abundance of seeds, if you had ragweed in Year One, you would anticipate more ragweed in Year Two. Instead, I found a solid carpet of a more attractive weed, marestail, and almost no ragweed at all.

It seemed a joke, played on me by the Powers. "Well, old John thinks he's smart enough to understand the mysteries of range ecology, so we'll give him solid marestail, just to keep him on his toes."

I noticed a change in the mix of trees around and below Moonshine Springs, and it occurred to me that I was witnessing a changing of the guard, a process that will alter the ecology of the canyon for decades to come . . . or until the next big fire deals a new hand of cards.

Before the fire, the old-guard cedars had ruled the area around Moonshine Springs for at least a century, their thick canopy shading out other trees that might have prospered around the springs. A few big elms and cottonwoods had fought their way to sunlight and had managed to survive into full growth, but they too had died in the fire.

Moonshine Springs had doubled or tripled its flow, and the spring pools I had noticed in the fall of 2017 were still there. Along this necklace of spring pools I saw three-foot sprouts of cottonwood and willow, and on the higher ground, away from the water, soapberry trees by the thousands.

With an open sky and sunlight, new vegetation was moving into the territory once ruled by the mighty cedars.

The following summer, in 2020, I noticed further changes. The ragweed and marestail had disappeared and a thick carpet of grass had sprung up on both sides of the springs. These were tall grasses I didn't recognize, not the gramas and buffalo grass we're accustomed to or even Old World bluestem. One of the new varieties resembled tall green wheat.

Grapevines and skunkbush sumac were prospering in the post-cedar era, as was a type of vegetation I had never seen before, a vine that was climbing on dead cedar trunks and branches. I was able to identify the plant as climbing milkweed vine (*Funastrum cynanchoides*). It occurs in Texas,

Oklahoma, New Mexico, Arizona, and California and needs full sun. Once established, it produces abundant seed and thrives, spreading along the ground and climbing trees.

Gardeners consider it a pest, but I think we will enjoy having it around. It will provide ground cover and will likely entertain Monarch butterflies on their annual migrations (https://davesgarden.com/guides/pf/go/136407/). In August, the vines yielded beautiful white puffy flowers that drew bees and butterflies. Those graceful flowers, draped on dead trees, seemed a perfect symbol of new life and rebirth.

The fire dramatically changed this little ecosystem. I predict that in ten years, the areas on both sides of the creek will become a soapberry forest, with a line of vine-draped willows and cottonwoods along the creek bed. Without the fire, those trees and vines wouldn't have had a chance to prosper.

FLOODING

Once the rains started in May 2019, the cycle continued as storm after storm moved across the northeastern Panhandle. We finished the month of May with an incredible 14 inches of rain, making it the wettest month since I started keeping records in 2002.

I checked the records for Perryton's rainfall, going back to 1900; they showed the average rainfall in May at three inches and the wettest month on record (July 1950) at 13.49". We had surpassed Perryton's wettest month of the past 119 years.

Ranch folks celebrated green grass and pastures that had become vast quilts of wildflowers, but veterans of the fires of 2006 and 2017 were already thinking about the amount of fuel we would have standing for the fire season of 2020. We had acquired a mindset that divided the calendar into Fire Season and Everything Else.

But our most immediate concern was flooding. A four-inch rain on May 20 filled the big pond in Pickett Canyon and another inch and a half sent water roaring over the dam, which was also the only road to the construction site of our new house. The water eroded the backside of the dam and left a gash eight feet deep, cutting the road and making it impossible for workers to continue working. It was a lousy time to lose a road.

I sent Scot a picture of the gash. Never one to be intimidated by a disaster, he texted back, "We'll fix that."

The next day, he showed up at the ranch with a John Deere 750K dozer and his new Kubota mini trackhoe. A big Kenworth dump truck and CASE backhoe pulled up behind him. The sign on the door said, "J. B. Ham Contractors."

J. B. climbed out of the truck. His full brown beard and stocky build gave him the look of a bear, while his wrap-around sunglasses hid the kindness in his eyes and added a sinister note . . . maybe a bear who belonged to a motorcycle gang.

We shook hands and I said, "The last time I saw that truck, you were hauling off my house."

He laughed, and when J. B. laughed, you could hear him on the other side of the canyon. "From fire to flood. What a world!"

For the next two days, Scot pushed dirt to provide fill for the crevice in the dam. J. B. moved his equipment to a caliche pit in the upper west pasture and hauled loads of caliche down the steep hill. The air was heavy with humidity, and Gulf clouds floated overhead. It rained every night.

Scot used "the mini," as he called the Kubota, to deepen the cut in the dam in order to drop the water level down to a certain depth, then installed a huge galvanized steel culvert, 5' x 40', that would drain the pond before it got close to breaching the dam. "That will never happen again," he said, and I'll bet it won't.

So the cycle of life returned to our world. We had survived the bomb cyclone, the fury of March, and the floods of May. The winds calmed and the ranch transformed into a fireworks pageant, revealing the geometry and colors of millions of wildflowers displayed against a backdrop of solid green.

The same day that a crew of workers poured the concrete footing for our new house, a swallow returned to her mud nest on the porch of my writing office. She will repair the nest and raise another batch of chicks. We will build another house and try again.

PART 2

A BROADER VIEW OF WILDFIRES

CHAPTER 7

A History of Fires in the Panhandle and South Plains

MY TASK IN PART 1 of this book was to present one man's observations of two very large, destructive prairie fires that swept through my home region of Texas. In part 2, I will draw on written sources, as well as my own experience, and try to place the fires of 2006 and 2017 into a broader perspective.

The 2017 fire brought home the fact that I knew very little about prairie fires, so I began acquiring books and doing research. I learned that fire has been a constant reality on the Southern Plains. The prairie is a sea of grass, and it has always burned.

In prehistoric times, some of the fires were touched off by lightning, but most were set by humans, intentional burns. Prehistoric people appear to have understood that they couldn't escape fire entirely, so they figured out how to manage it.

"Whenever primitive man has had the opportunity to turn fire loose on a land, he seems to have done so, from time immemorial. . . . That they burned methodically can hardly be doubted. . . . It is only civilized societies that have undertaken to stop fires" (Pyne 2017, 20–21).

They burned grass in the spring, knowing that the new growth would attract deer and bison. They used fire to drive bison to killing zones and as a weapon of warfare—offensively to destroy an enemy and defensively to elude pursuers. Whether intended or not, this burning cleansed the grasslands of invader brush and trees and reduced the chance of catastrophic wildfires.

So did the grazing patterns of millions of bison. Bison herds often grazed the prairie vegetation right into the ground, so that detachments of the United States Army couldn't find grazing for their mules and horses. In 1882, the explorer Randolph B. Marcy reported no firewood in a space of 600 miles on the Southern Plains. His group made their cooking fires with buffalo chips and sunflower stalks (Hart and Hart 1997, 6, 8).

On the presettlement prairie, a fire had little chance of becoming a megafire. Billy Dixon saw the plains of Kansas, Oklahoma, Texas, and Colorado in the late 1860s when bison were still plentiful. "The grass that grew in the Plains did not have the height to produce a sweeping, high rolling fire, such as was often seen in regions of the tall bluestem in Eastern Kansas" (Dixon 1987, 53).

But the fire equation on the Southern Plains underwent a dramatic change around 1878. The bison herds had been exterminated. The Kiowas, Comanches, Southern Cheyenne, and Arapahos had been moved to reservation lands in Indian Territory and were no longer burning the prairie. When the region received abundant rain, it transformed into an ocean of vegetation.

In *Prairie Gothic*, I record the memories of J. W. Hunt, who settled in the village of Estacado, Texas, near present-day Lubbock, in 1880, the same year my great-great-grandparents arrived: "With vast wonder, we beheld the virgin land. No plow had ever depraved its sod. . . . Copious rains had fallen. The prairie grass, lush and green, covered the land. . . . The landscape, dotted with little lakes gleaming in the morning sun, seemed a vast emerald shield embossed with gems and silver" (Erickson 2005, 16).

Ranchers from downstate clambered to move cattle into this expanse of grass, but it was a slow process. For a period of about twenty years, the entire Southern Plains were understocked and loaded with fuel. "There were 2.4 million cattle on the Plains in 1880 and 7.5 million in 1885. When these numbers are compared to the number of bison that the grassland had previously supported . . . the Plains were 'relatively understocked' even in 1885. . . . A dense fuel source in turn almost certainly led to more intense and dangerous prairie fires" (Courtwright 2011, 74).

Settlers and cowboys brought matches, campfires, cigarettes . . . and prairie fires. Tobacco-related fires became such a problem on the XIT ranch, management established strict rules about smoking on ranch property, which caused much grumbling among the cowboys.

In his book on the XIT, J. Evetts Haley left us a good record of prairie fires in the last two decades of the nineteenth century (Haley 1953, 169–81; also see Haley 1929, 23–42). In its prime, the XIT covered over three million acres, a strip of land that began near present-day Dalhart on the north and ran all the way down to the South Plains, west of today's Lubbock.

It was all virgin prairie and it burned—hot, fierce, and out of control. Haley noted that most or all of the big fires between 1879 and 1900 were caused by human carelessness, not by lightning or intentional burning.

The XIT management expected their cowboys to fight every fire, and they did it with the primitive tools at hand: shovels, wet gunnysacks, brooms, saddle blankets, and slickers. Sometimes they lit backfires. Sometimes they would kill a beef, peel back half the hide, and drag it with horses on both sides of a line of fire. Later, if events permitted, they dined on the barbecued beef.

Some of these fires were huge and wind-driven, and cowboy firefighters stayed out of the way. A fire in the winter of 1884 began on the Cimarron River in southwestern Kansas, north of the XIT range, and burned almost a hundred miles to the south through the ranch, torching over a million acres until a blizzard stopped it near the Canadian River. Another fire struck the XIT's Canadian River country in 1885, and another came in 1887 on the south end of the ranch.

In 1894, another fire, "one of the worst," started in New Mexico and moved into Texas, pushed by a strong west wind. It burned for weeks, and ranch employees calculated that a swath of XIT land almost twenty by sixty miles had been burned clean of grass. That figure didn't include any grassland lost in New Mexico or on other Texas ranches.

Haley didn't give a specific number of acres consumed in that fire, and estimates vary, but some scholars believe that it burned over six million acres—"one of the largest fires ever to burn in North America" (Lindley 2017, 3).

Haley mentioned a fire in June 1879 that occurred before the founding of the XIT. It started in Crosby County and might have been "the most destructive prairie fire to have swept the South Plains." Hank Smith, one of the first settlers in Crosby County, recalled that it moved to the northeast and burned thousands of square miles of country.

Another bad fire swept Crosby County in 1898. This one burned within a mile of the town of Emma, and residents turned out to fight it. Burning cow chips and tumbleweeds rolled ahead of the blaze, starting fires beneath the floors of buildings and setting roofs ablaze, but the town survived.*

Haley's research indicates that the last twenty-one years of the nineteenth century saw prairie fires in 1879, 1884, 1885, 1887, 1894, and 1898, and at least four of them were comparable in size and ferocity to the ones we experienced in 2006 and 2017. But the fire equation shifted around 1900, making the West Texas prairie less vulnerable to huge fires. Increasing numbers of cattle grazed off excess grass, and farmers began breaking out the prairie sod into farmland. Plowed fields and roads became fireguards, stopping fires before they grew into massive blazes. As the population increased, so did efforts at fire suppression.

That condition prevailed through most of the twentieth century. My parents and grandparents told stories about blizzards, droughts, and dust storms in West Texas, but not monster wildfires. I began working on ranches as a boy in 1957, but until 2006, I had never witnessed a megafire or had even heard the term. Neither had other ranchers in my region.

It appears to me that by 2006, the fire equation had shifted, putting our ornaments of civilization into the path of very large and destructive megafires. What had changed?

---

* For more information about early wildfires on West Texas and eastern New Mexico ranches, see Willie Newbury Lewis, *Tapadero: The Making of a Cowboy*, Austin: University of Texas Press, 1972; W. C. Holden, *Rollie Burns*, College Station: Texas A&M University Press, 1932 and 1986; and Vivian H. Whitlock, *Cowboy Life on the Llano Estacado*, Norman: University of Oklahoma Press, 1970.

CHAPTER 8

Why Prairie Fires Now?

SO WHY WERE WE VISITED by these two mammoth fires in a span of eleven years, and what had changed? Here are some of my speculations.

AN INCREASE IN POPULATION

Prehistoric people set fires and wandered around immense landscapes. Modern societies extinguish fires and live in permanent structures. The settlers who poured into the prairie states after the Civil War brought Euro-American ideas about private ownership of land. They built homes, barns, ranch fencing, and businesses that they didn't want to lose in a fire and increased their efforts to extinguish fires as quickly as possible.

In 1880, when my great-great-grandparents arrived in the village of Estacado, the population of the entire Texas Panhandle and South Plains was probably less than five hundred. Today, that region has a population of more than a million people, brought in and sustained by the oil industry, irrigation agriculture, cattle feeding, wind energy, and the commercial ventures that have grown up around those core industries.

Every little town in West Texas has a volunteer fire department, and cities such as Midland, Lubbock, Abilene, San Angelo, and Amarillo spend millions of dollars each year to maintain a well-equipped militia of professionals who are trained to fight fires.

They are brave and efficient, but their job is getting harder, because more people have brought more opportunities for starting fires: trains, welding rigs, cutting torches, campfires, vehicle exhaust, cigarette butts, fireworks, downed power lines, and things you would never think about, such as a lawnmower blade striking a rock, a spark from the exhaust of a chainsaw, or a chain dragging off the back of a truck.

Fire scholar Stephen Pyne points out that the way we live in present-day America has placed us on a collision course with nature. Ecological checks and balances are scrambled or blurred, and "wildfires spread through the landscape like rats in a plague city. We're witnessing fires that exceed anything we've seen before" (Pyne 2017, 4, 22–23, 137).

THE INCREASE OF ELECTRICAL SERVICE IN RURAL AREAS

In 2017, the northern half of Roberts County had a population of about twenty people. Electric power didn't show up here until the 1960s, when the oil industry created a demand for service. If that hadn't occurred, we might not have electricity today.

Isolated ranches and oil field locations in Roberts, Hemphill, Lipscomb, and Ochiltree Counties receive their electrical service through a network of poles and lines provided by our rural electric cooperative, North Plains Electric, headquartered in Perryton. Residents of other counties in the Panhandle receive their service through Xcel Energy or small electric cooperatives.

Each power company maintains hundreds of miles of above-ground lines, poles, transformers, and substations, in a weather environment that can only be described as hostile. The system is exposed to lightning strikes, tornadoes, ice storms, strong prevailing winds, and winds that sometimes gust to hurricane force.

The companies do their best to upgrade the system and maintain power to every customer, but on any given day in the Panhandle, there might be one pole, cross-arm, or insulator in those hundreds of miles of power lines that will break under the strain of a sixty mile an hour wind.

The formula that produced the massive fires of 2006 and 2017 was this: an accumulation of fuel after a wet summer + a dry winter + low humidity + extremely high wind + a spark produced by a breakdown in the electrical system. When those conditions are present, the question is not IF a fire will break out but where, when, and how bad.

The thought occurred to me that when the National Weather Service issues a Red Flag Warning for fire, maybe rural electrical cooperatives should shut down the system in high-risk areas during the hours of greatest fire danger, usually between 11 a.m. and 8 p.m. That seemed a sensible idea until the fire season of 2018, when we endured months of heightened fire alerts, not just a few worrisome days.

Clearly, shutting down the electrical system for months at a time is not likely to happen. We are addicted to electricity and the conveniences it brings, and the dark side of the bargain is that we make ourselves more vulnerable to fire.

CHANGES IN GRAZING PATTERNS AND AGRICULTURAL PRACTICES

The droughts of the 1930s and 1950s left an indelible scar on the American mind, a vivid memory of what drought and wind can do to prairie that has been broken out into farmland.

Starting in the 1950s, the USDA's Soil Bank and Conservation Reserve Programs brought significant changes to range conditions in the Panhandle and South Plains. Under those programs, farmers received payments for taking marginal farmland out of production and seeding it back to grass, which made good sense from several angles.

First, the grass reduced wind and water erosion on unproductive farm ground and increased the soil's ability to hold and absorb rain water. When the land came out of the Soil Bank and CRP programs, the tall grasses produced more forage per acre than the short native grasses and provided landowners with good summer grazing plus a source of winter hay.

Second, taller, non-native species of grass such as Old World bluestem and sand lovegrass made excellent cover and habitat for wildlife. Mule deer, whitetail deer, pronghorn antelope, wild turkey, pheasant, and quail have prospered as a result. When I worked on the Ellzey ranch in the 1970s, we rarely saw deer along Wolf Creek. Today, they are plentiful, both whitetails and mule deer.

But these conservation programs have also removed hundreds of thousands of fire-safe acres (plowed fields) and turned them into hundreds of thousands of acres of tall standing fuel. Our native shortgrass prairie has been transformed into a partial-tallgrass prairie that resembles the tallgrass country in the Kansas Flint Hills and the Osage region of northeastern Oklahoma.

Ranchers in those regions burn their grass every spring through controlled burning, a tradition that began decades ago. We have no such tradition here in Texas. After a dry winter, those fields of tall CRP grass are almost explosive. As the Perryton fire of 2017 moved eastward from its point of ignition, it found abundant fuel in thousands of acres of tall CRP grass in Lipscomb and Hemphill Counties, and those counties suffered the heaviest loss of livestock.

Christopher Collins, writing in the *Texas Observer*, pointed out that little research has been done on the relationship between CRP land and fire danger. One of the few studies, a conference paper authored by National Weather Service meteorologist Todd Lindley, found a correlation between conservation programs and fire danger. "'What you get is this turn back to the natural landscape, which was historically a landscape where fire was very prevalent'" (Collins 2017, 1).

Since the drought of 2011–2014, I have noticed clumps of Old World bluestem (CRP grass) appearing on our ranch. It is coming up on disturbed ground, in ditches, and on the side of roads, but also in pastures that have always been dominated by shorter native grasses. In the pasture, it appears in circles that are easy to spot, foliage that is taller than the native grasses and a paler shade of green.

I assume that the seeds either have been brought in by wind or birds from CRP fields four or five miles north of us or have come from bales of hay we fed the cattle during the 2011 drought and after the 2017 fire.

I don't know if we should welcome this change or regard the new grass as an invader. On the one hand, Old World bluestem is a palatable grass in spring and early summer. Cattle do well on it, and it produces a lot of vertical forage. On the other hand, in late summer and fall it becomes too coarse for cattle and goes into winter with a twelve-to-eighteen-inch profile.

In a dry winter and spring, that high profile becomes fuel for a fire.

In September 2017, I made a trip to Amarillo and saw Old World bluestem growing in the ditches on both sides of the highway, all the way from the Canadian River to the east side of Amarillo, a distance of about ninety miles. August rains had brought full growth, and every stalk held hundreds of seeds. You could have baled hay all the way from the Canadian River Bridge to the Amarillo airport.

In that stretch of highway, Old World bluestem had become the dominant form of vegetation in the ditches, and that was something I had not seen before. Like it or not, we are becoming a semi-tallgrass prairie, and fire-weary ranchers hope the Texas Department of Transportation has money in the budget to mow the ditches before the next fire season.

INVASIVE BRUSH

Another change I have observed in my lifetime is the increase of brush in the form of mesquite, juniper, cedar, Russian olive, and salt cedar. Our efforts to control prairie fires have protected these species and allowed them to proliferate.

Archeologists working on my ranch have found evidence of red cedar and one-seed juniper in sites that date to AD 1300, so we know those species were present in prehistoric times, but farmers and ranchers on the plains have planted them in shelter belts around country homes, often obtaining the trees through conservation programs sponsored by the USDA. They are popular trees on the plains because they are hearty and resistant to drought. Birds have spread the seeds, and now they not only compete with native plants but also bring a dramatic increase of fuel for the next wildfire.

WEATHER AND CLIMATE

Many experts are convinced that for decades, the earth has experienced a pattern of rising temperature that has increased the frequency and severity of wildfires. The cause of the warming has become a matter of fierce debate: Is this man-made climate *change* or a natural climate *variation*?

Katharine Hayhoe, a climate scientist and director of the Climate Science Center at Texas Tech, says, "Today, there is no legitimate national or international scientific organization that does not accept the fundamental role of humans as drivers of recent climate change" (Hayhoe and Farley 2009, 70).

Christopher Monckton, once a policy adviser to British Prime Minister Margaret Thatcher and now the chief policy adviser at the Science and Public Policy Institute in Virginia, argues that "there is no—and I mean no—scientific basis for the exaggerated predictions of future global warming" (Kent Covington interview, *WORLD* magazine, July 8, 2014).

It is difficult for the average citizen to sort this out. Where is the science and where is the politics? We must hope that the people trained in climate research are asking good questions and producing honest work and that the public can figure out how to use their information.

B. A. Stewart, a soil scientist at West Texas A&M University, studied precipitation and temperature data in a 39-county region in West Texas and concluded that between 1895 and 2013, the area became significantly warmer, while precipitation declined slightly. He didn't attribute this alteration to any particular cause but said his findings were consistent with global patterns recorded by other scientists (*Texas Climate News*, May 15, 2014). In a letter to me, he added:

> I am 100% sure that no scientific study will ever
> definitively answer what the full effect of man's
> activity is having on the climate, but we cannot dis-
> pute the fact that temperatures are rising and it does
> have an effect on grass fires. Politics did not cause
> the increase in temperature. Landowners must deal
> with the change regardless of the cause. (Letter to
> the author, September 2017, used with permission.)

If temperatures are indeed rising, that is bad news for those of us on the Southern Plains.

I would add another observation to the discussion of weather and climate. It appears to me that in the years since 2000, we have seen a shift in moisture patterns: an increase of rainfall during the summer growing season and a decrease of snowfall in the late winter.

Snow is nature's most effective fire suppressant. When it is present on the prairie landscape, nothing burns. When it melts, most of the moisture goes into soil and plants rather than gushing down ditches and ravines and collecting in ponds. In 2006 and 2017, when Texas saw the biggest wild-fires in historical memory, we received no significant snowfall.

Any rancher who has been feeding cattle in my part of Texas for the past four decades can testify that we received more snow in the 1970s, 1980s, and 1990s than in recent decades. Our annual moisture totals might have remained the same or even gone up (totals in Perryton for both 2006 and 2017 were above the 21" average), but the distribution of moisture has increased the amount of standing fuel (tall grass) while removing the protection of fire-suppressing snow in the critical month of March, the wildest and windiest month of the year. Together, they have magnified our vulnerability to wildfires.

This argument is based on anecdotal evidence and doesn't qualify as hard science, but I'm not the only rancher who has noticed what appears to be a relationship between snow and fire.

CHAPTER 9

The Management of Fire

FOR A VARIETY OF REASONS, large destructive fires seem to have become a fact of life for those of us who live on the Great Plains. For generations, we've considered fire an enemy and a threat. Until recent years, we've assumed that we could conquer it with technology, as we have controlled polio and smallpox. The fire seasons since 2006 have caused us to wonder about that.

Stephen J. Pyne is convinced that our effort to suppress natural fires has increased our vulnerability to the kind of monsters we saw in 2006 and 2017:

> The issue is whether [fire] will return as conflagration or as a conservation practice. . . . An obvious solution is to burn off that surplus [fuel] under controlled conditions, which would reduce the risk of wildfire and enhance the long-suffering grasses. But fire management also requires intellectual and political space.

Fire must be seen . . . as a useful process (Pyne 2017, 6, 132).

Pyne is saying that we must start looking for "good smoke" and figure out how to coexist with fire. He is not alone in this argument, nor the first to make it. For at least two generations, professors of range management at academic institutions like Texas A&M, Texas Tech, Kansas State, and Oklahoma State have been arguing the benefits of fire and urging landowners to use it, not only to protect their property but because the prairie needs fire to sustain native grasses and control the spread of invader plants.

Most ranchers take pride in caring for the land and want to leave it better for the next generation. We might not call ourselves environmentalists, but we are. Even so, in my part of the world, landowners continue to resist controlled burning. Why?

Well, we're not joiners and aren't always friendly to change. As a people, we are very traditional in our thinking, tied to the slow patterns of land and animals and dedicated to management techniques we learned from older ranchers, parents, and grandparents.

The arguments in favor of prescribed burning often come across as a slap at our stewardship of the land; traditional grazing practices (without fire) are damaging the ecology of the prairie we revere. That might be true—I believe it is—but it's hard to accept in a graceful manner.

Another reason that landowners have been slow to embrace prescribed burning is that, to put it in blunt terms, we have to worry about getting sued. For generations, farmers and ranchers on the plains have divided land into surveyors' units (township, section, half-section, quarter-section, and acres), and each unit of property is owned by someone who has invested money in fencing and improvements.

Fire doesn't recognize our legal descriptions and goes where it will. If a controlled burn on my ranch gets out of hand, it might destroy tens of thousands of acres around me, miles of barbed wire fence, livestock, the homes of neighbors, and, God forbid, someone's husband, wife, or child.

Somewhere in Dallas and Austin, law firms are watching the news for such reports and they will be in touch. Does my ranch insurance policy cover that kind of liability? Who thinks to ask?

A weird twist to this situation might be that eventually the lawyers will come from the opposite direction. If wildfires continue to plague the prairie states, we might see the day when landowners get sued for *not* burning to control the buildup of grass, weeds, and brush.

For generations, landowners in my region have viewed all grass fires as bad smoke and bad news. We have resisted prescribed burning because we have a primordial, brain-stem reaction to the scent of burning grass and to billows of white smoke on the horizon. We are terrified of fire and the destruction it can bring.

Dr. Ron Sosebee told me a funny story about Dr. Henry Wright, a professor in the Range Management Department at Texas Tech and an early and fervent advocate of prescribed burning of rangeland. The latter spoke one time to a gathering of ranchers. The next day, the chairman of the department got a call from an angry member of the audience: "I don't know if you're aware of this, Sir, but you've got a pyromaniac on your faculty!"

In another context, Dr. Wright explained that prescribed burning isn't as dangerous as most people think, "providing that it is being done by experienced personnel. We recommend a minimum of 2 years of prescribed burning experience under a range of weather conditions. . . . To achieve a desired effect and for safety, one must have the skill to recognize, and the patience to wait for favorable weather" (Wright and Bailey 1980, 5).

There are people who know how to do this, and they do it on a regular basis. Some are on the faculty of land-grant universities and some are private contractors. Several months before the 2006 fires, I had a conversation with such a man. He was an advocate of controlled burning of ranchland, had participated in many burns, and held certification that allowed him to do it.

He made a compelling argument that burning was an important, even necessary, tool for managing ranch land. The prairie needed and benefitted from periodic burning. I was persuaded, and we discussed the possibility of doing some controlled burns on my ranch in the spring.

Then came the fires in March and all talk of controlled burns came to a screeching halt. Anyone who had dropped a match into dry grass would have become extremely unpopular with ranchers and firefighters who had watched the 2006 fire rampage across 900,000 acres of Panhandle grassland. We had been branded with a hot iron, and it left us with a deep fear of smoke and flames.

Those of us who operate ranches in big prairie country, such as the Canadian River Valley, might recognize the importance of prescribed burning but wonder if it will work in our rugged terrain. Deep canyons take most firefighting equipment out of the equation: graders, dozers, fire trucks, and tanker trucks. Canyons do weird things to wind currents, and most canyons contain a large population of cedar and juniper.

Nobody wants to be the test case for prescribed burning in rough terrain.

That is unfortunate, because the arguments in favor of prescribed burning remain just as strong today as they were in

2006—stronger, in fact, because these fires continue to crash against us like waves against a rocky coast. One hates to think the trend can continue, but it certainly might.

The estrangement of civilized beings from nature is a theme that goes back nearly five thousand years to the *Epic of Gilgamesh*. We are stewards of our resources but also intruders. We love the land but can't avoid changing it, simply by living on it and using it. My family and I want to live in harmony with our land and to be part of its natural rhythms, but we're not always sure how to accomplish that goal.

The part of my brain that reads books on fire ecology is trying to whisper soothing words to the part that doesn't like the smell of smoke. We haven't worked it out yet, but at least we're talking.

CHAPTER 10

Afterthoughts

ONE CONSISTENT QUALITY IN HUMAN beings is that we are prone to second-guess important decisions, even when we know it's a futile exercise. Two years after the fire of 2017, I was still waking up in the middle of the night, reassessing the decision I made at approximately three o'clock on the afternoon of March 6 to evacuate our house and leave with only what we could carry.

Hindsight had brought the luxury of a calmer perspective. It's likely that the flames didn't touch our property until 5:30 or 6 that evening, when the wind shifted to the north and sent the fire into Pickett Canyon. Up to that time, it was roaring across the flats north of our place, in a southwest-to-northeast direction, away from our ranch and toward Lipscomb County.

Kris and I might have had two hours to spray water on the house, the bunkhouse, and my office. We might have saved the structures. We could have loaded the car with things we didn't want to lose: the dogs, my two banjos, Kris's quilts and scrapbooks, photographs, books, and some clothes.

A man with long experience in prescribed burning told me, "If I'd been in your shoes, I would have left a long trail of burning matches on the way out." In other words, he would have tried to start backfires that might have saved our structures. You start small fires that might stop the big one. That was probably excellent advice, but it would have required a kind of steely self-discipline I didn't have. On March 6, 2017, lighting fires was the last thing on my mind.

In lucid moments, I *know* that dropping everything and leaving the ranch was the right call. The wildfire of 2006 had given us a frightening example of what megafires can do. Twelve people died in that fire, most of them trapped and overwhelmed by a kind of firestorm they had never seen before. If you make the wrong decision in that kind of fire, you pay a terrible price.

I've heard several versions of how quickly wildfires can move. J. Evetts Haley reported cases of fires traveling as fast as a man on horseback (Haley 1953, 174). A resident in nineteenth century Kansas said that a fire could move at the speed of a railroad train (Courtwright 2011, 110). A rancher who went through the 2006 fire said that a wildfire moves at half the speed of the wind, which means that a fire driven by a 60-mph wind will cover a mile in two minutes.

A deputy sheriff told me that a helicopter pilot clocked the 2017 fire on the flats in Ochiltree County at seventy miles per hour. Is that possible? One of the things I've heard about that fire is that it generated such intense heat, grass and cedar trees were igniting *before* the flames got there, as if by magic.

A number of people had near-miss experiences in the 2017 fire. The common theme was they thought they had time to move livestock, load the dogs, or save precious items from the house. Then, suddenly, the fire was on top of them, a pall of dark smoke that left them blind, disoriented, and gasping for air.

Then came a wall of heat. Tanja Bussard at Lipscomb said it almost knocked her down. She was lucky that Lance, her husband, was in his pickup and found her. She was able to see his headlights in the smoke. Lance and Tanja are good friends of ours. They lost cattle and were fortunate to survive.

One of our neighbors up on the flats was caught in the same situation, trying to move cattle out of danger. He saved himself by diving into a stock tank.

As I noted earlier, my greatest fear on the afternoon of March 6 was not the fire we could see to the north but the fires we *couldn't* see, the ones that might be coming from the west and southwest, upwind of us. There were hundreds of miles of power lines in the northeastern Panhandle, and on the afternoon of March 6, one of them broke under the stress of powerful winds and started the Perryton fire. There might have been others ready to break.

In a moment of crisis, we make rapid decisions and live with the consequences. If we were faced with the same circumstances today, I would make the same decision: flee and don't look back. The hard part is not looking back.

Bibliography

Collins, Christopher. "Fanning the Flames." www.texasob-server.org, August 21, 2017.

Courtwright, Julie. *Prairie Fire: A Great Plains History.* Lawrence: University of Kansas Press, 2011.

Covington, Kent. "The World and Everything in It." *WORLD* magazine, July 8, 2014.

Dixon, Olive K. *The Life of Billy Dixon.* Abilene, TX: State House Press, 1987.

Erickson, John R. *Prairie Gothic: One Family's Story in West Texas.* Denton: University of North Texas Press, 2005.

Haley, J. Evetts. *Charles Goodnight: Cowman and Plainsman,* new edition. Norman: University of Oklahoma Press, 1949.

———. "Grass Fires of the Southern Plains." *West Texas Historical Association Yearbook*, vol. V. Lubbock: WTHA Publications, 1929, 23–42.

———. *The XIT Ranch of Texas and the Early Days of the Llano Estacado.* Norman: University of Oklahoma Press, 1953.

Hart, Richard H., and James A. Hart. "Rangelands of the Great Plains Before European Settlement." *Rangelands* 19 (February 1997): 6–8.

Hayhoe, Katharine, and Andrew Farley. *A Climate for Change: Global Warming Facts for Faith-Based Decisions.* Franklin,

TN: FaithWords Publishing, 2009.

Hollandsworth, Skip. "Love and Loss on the Plains: The Day the Fire Came to the Franklin Ranch." *Texas Monthly*, August 2017.

Kodas, Michael. *Megafire: A Race to Extinguish a Deadly Epidemic of Flame*. New York: Houghton Mifflin Harcourt, 2017.

Lindley, Todd. "Firestorm: Notes and Observations from the 6 March 2017 Southern Great Plains Wildfire Outbreak." Norman, Oklahoma: National Weather Service, 2017.

Pyne, Stephen J. *The Great Plains: A Fire Survey*. Tucson: University of Arizona Press, 2017.

———*Fire: Nature and Culture*. London: Reaktion Books, 2012.

———*Between Two Fires: A Fire History of Contemporary America*. Tucson: University of Arizona Press, 2012.

Texas Climate News. "West Texas A&M Analysis: Panhandle Became Warmer, Drier From 1895–2013." May 15, 2014. http://texasclimatenews.org/?p=9504

Wright, Henry A., and Arthur W. Bailey. "Fire Ecology and Prescribed Burning in the Great Plains—A Research Review." *USDA Forest Service General Technical Report INT-77*, May 1980.

Index

About the Author

Photo courtesy of *Western Horseman* magazine

JOHN R. ERICKSON, one-time bartender, handyman, cowboy, and founder of Maverick Books, has written and published 75 books and more than 600 articles. He is the author of the bestselling Hank the Cowdog series of books, audiobooks, and stage plays. His writing has garnered many accolades, including the Audie, Oppenheimer, Wrangler, and Lamplighter Awards, and his works have been translated into Spanish, Danish, Farsi, and Chinese. A fifth-generation Texan, Erickson owns a ranch in Perryton, Texas.